IQ A PRACTICAL GUIDE TO INQUIRY-BASED LEARNING

IQ A PRACTICAL GUIDE TO INQUIRY-BASED LEARNING

JENNIFER WATT AND JILL COLYER

OXFORD
UNIVERSITY PRESS

OXFORD
UNIVERSITY PRESS

Oxford University Press is a department of the University of Oxford.
It furthers the University's objective of excellence in research, scholarship,
and education by publishing worldwide. Oxford is a registered trade mark of
Oxford University Press in the UK and in certain other countries.

Published in Canada by
Oxford University Press
8 Sampson Mews, Suite 204,
Don Mills, Ontario M3C 0H5 Canada

www.oupcanada.com

Library and Archives Canada Cataloguing in Publication
Watt, Jennifer Gail, 1965–, author
IQ : a practical guide to inquiry-based learning / Jennifer
Watt and Jill Colyer.

Includes bibliographical references and index.
ISBN 978-0-19-900934-3 (pbk.)

1. Inquiry-based learning. 2. Teaching. I. Colyer, Jill, author
II. Title. III. Title: Practical guide to inquiry-based learning.

LB1027.23.W28 2014   **371.39**   **C2013-907971-8**

Cover images: © Alex Belomlinsky/iStockphoto; © ARTQU/iStockPhoto;
© RBFried/iStockphoto; © Mr_Vector/iStockphoto

The publisher has endeavoured to meet or exceed industry specifications in the
manufacturing of this textbook. The spine of this sewn book has been reinforced
for specially designed fabric for extra binding strength. The cover is premium,
polymer-reinforced material designed to provide long life and withstand daily
classroom use. Mylar gloss lamination has been applied for durability.

Printed and bound in Canada

7 — 16 15

Oxford University Press is committed to our environment.
This book is printed on Forest Stewardship Council® certified paper, harvested from a
responsibly managed forest.

CONTENTS

Chapter 6 – Synthesize, Evaluate, and Draw Conclusions

Chapter 7 – In Closing

Reproducibles

FOREWORD

In my first year of teaching, I faced the daunting prospect of evaluation by the principal. I *delivered* a lesson in which I talked for most of the seventy minutes while my students dutifully sat, listened, and behaved. When called upon, selected students answered my predictable questions. The principal was impressed. "That was comparable to a lesson delivered by my most experienced teachers," he said. All was well—until I found myself surplus to the school's requirements after one year!

My next assignment was at a composite high school serving large numbers of challenged—and challenging!—students. Suddenly talking *at* students for seventy minutes didn't work; assigning homework was futile. For the next few weeks I struggled and floundered. Eventually, with some invaluable mentoring from experienced colleagues, I changed my approach. They suggested that I talk less and listen more. I experimented with inviting students to pose their own questions; I tried to discover each of their interests; I sought to engage them by connecting learning to their world.

During the next five years, I slowly and painstakingly had to discover for myself the same wisdom that informs this wonderful new resource, *IQ: A Practical Guide to Inquiry-based Learning*: namely that learning is about curiosity, discovery, uncertainty, argument, passion, and individuality.

If one examines curriculum documents across Canada, *critical thinking* heads the lists of essential skills. Yet ironically, these same documents have become increasingly prescriptive regarding what teachers *must* teach and what students *must* learn. This appears to be a mixed message, especially to beginning teachers. *IQ* addresses this conundrum directly, reminding us, in the words of Grant Wiggins, that deep learning is about students "uncovering understanding," not teachers *covering* endless lists of learning outcomes.

Every week, I invite teachers to challenge the curriculum, to discuss learning outcomes and expectations, and to ask, "Are these worthy targets for learning? Do they demand that students think? Do they suggest a diversity of opinion, or do they encourage rote compliance to the status quo?" *IQ* reminds us that teaching and learning must focus emphatically upon thinking, that knowledge and understanding are radically different from each other, that deep, sustainable learning does *not* occur as the result of a single lesson but requires that students wrestle with differing perspectives and points of view, argue with each other, make mistakes, take wrong turns, and eventually come to understand concepts, theories, beliefs, histories, herstories, and their own stories.

Beyond its solid pedagogical philosophy, *IQ* is rich in concrete material that will support teachers in improving their practice. Case studies illustrate how teachers can rely less upon closed questions designed to reveal declarative knowledge in favour of rich inquiry questions. A similar, scaffolded approach helps teachers guide *students* to pose increasingly rich, thoughtful inquiry questions. The authors also provide explanations and clear examples illustrating how existing units of study may be revised in order to engage students through rich inquiry.

After decades of neglect, assessment is now seen as being equal in importance to curriculum when teachers are planning their programs. The groundbreaking work of Grant Wiggins, Jay McTighe, and Dylan Wiliam provides the foundation for the assessment philosophy of *IQ*. Hence, the authors draw on the latest research, which makes a compelling case for balancing formative with summative assessment, for clarity about the purpose and primary user of each kind of assessment, and for much greater involvement of students in their own assessment.

Reading *IQ* will inspire new teachers to place thinking at the centre of their teaching; it will assist seasoned teachers in re-examining their programs to foster greater relevance and engagement; but its greatest legacy will be to ensure that students rediscover the childlike excitement that accompanies rich, authentic, meaningful learning.

—Damian Cooper

Author of *Talk About Assessment: Strategies and Tools to Improve Learning* (2007), *Talk About Assessment: High School Strategies and Tools* (2010), and *Redefining Fair: How to Plan, Assess, and Grade for Excellence in Mixed-Ability Classrooms* (2011).

ABOUT THE AUTHORS

JENNIFER WATT is an instructional leader for beginning teachers at the Toronto District School Board. She has been a history, politics, social science, and English teacher, and a consultant and coordinator for 25 years. Throughout her career, she has supported both new and experienced classroom teachers at all grade levels and subject areas in thinking about how to share their knowledge, experience, and practices to improve student learning and establish professional communities. She is the author of several books for teachers and students, as well as exemplars and curriculum units. Jennifer has a Master's Degree focusing on the assessment of teacher practice.

JILL COLYER is the national coordinator of The Historical Thinking Project, a pan-Canadian history education reform initiative that is working towards the incorporation of historical thinking concepts into curricula, classroom resources, and teacher supports. She works closely with ministries of education in each province and territory, advises educational publishers on resource development, and facilitates professional development workshops for teachers and administrators across the country. Jill has been a teacher and a writer of curriculum materials since 1991. Her current work in curriculum development includes the writing of courses, textbooks, teaching guides, and assessment tools.

ACKNOWLEDGEMENTS

Thanks to David, Monica, Jessica, Laura, and everyone at Oxford University Press for their tremendous support and skill in making this book come to life.

This book is dedicated to my daughter Emma who is gentle, funny, and wise.

It is also dedicated with tremendous gratitude to my husband Barry in appreciation of his generous nature, continual support, and wicked sense of humour. I extend much love to my sons Matt and Sean, my mother Joan, and my mother-in-law Marion. You make each day special.

Thanks to Jill, my co-author, for being both a good friend and collaborator.

Thank you to all the teachers I've had an opportunity to learn alongside. I am grateful for the opportunity to have had the rich conversations and to have shared the curiosities that ultimately shaped this book.

—Jennifer

I am grateful for all the educators across the country who have allowed me into their classrooms and schools and have shared their triumphs and challenges as they try to help students succeed. My experiences with these teachers and administrators continue to validate my firmly held belief in the power of education.

I would like to thank Peter Seixas for his intellectual and emotional generosity, for changing forever the way I see history, and for being the best boss in the world. And to Jennifer Watt, for being a great teacher and friend.

I am thankful for the unwavering support of my parents and my sisters and for the kindness of my friends—including the incredible community of women who kept me sane while trying to juggle the demands of motherhood and work.

To my sons Sam and Jack, who are the bright and shining lights in my heart. You make me grateful every day and remind me that we need to focus on teaching kids, not curriculum.

And to David, for filling my life with love, laughter, and tenderness. I am incredibly fortunate to get to share my life with you.

—Jill

CHAPTER 1
AN INTRODUCTION TO
INQUIRY

1.1 What is inquiry-based learning?

1.2 Why is inquiry-based learning effective?

1.3 What are various types of inquiry?

1.1

What is inquiry-based learning?

Human beings are born curious. From birth, we strive to make meaning of the world. We see this particularly in how young children ask questions and respond to what they are learning and how they are learning it. They can be simultaneously surprised, delighted, perplexed, and frustrated with new learning.

As teachers, we wonder what happens to that natural curiosity, which seems to be extinguished over time. We hope to reignite that early passion for learning in teenagers who may resist the desire to know more or to question what is.

Learning through inquiry is both a teaching method and a skill for students that harnesses natural curiosity and wonder. Inquiry-based learning has a long history in education. It is based on the notion that there are effective processes that can be used to solve problems, create new knowledge, resolve doubts, and find the truth. This type of learning can be explicitly taught so that both teachers and students consciously create classroom conditions that foster powerful inquiry.

If you are a teacher who would like to know more about the power of inquiry as a way to engage young people in making sense of the world through a disciplinary lens, then this book is for you.

IQ: A Practical Guide to Inquiry-based Learning:

- describes exactly what makes inquiry a better way of learning,
- identifies the qualities of a successful inquiry program, and
- shows what inquiry looks like as you and your students create an inquiry-centred classroom.

> **Learning through inquiry is both a teaching method and a skill for students that harnesses natural curiosity and wonder.**

Practical suggestions for planning, assessment, and teaching strategies are also provided. Key questions posed by teachers, case studies of teachers initiating inquiry-based learning, and quotes about inquiry methods are offered throughout to promote thinking and understanding of inquiry, and how it can be applied successfully to your classroom.

The key characteristics of inquiry-based learning

Inquiry-based learning is a process used to solve problems, create new knowledge, resolve doubts, and find the truth. Inquiry involves working with others and respecting a diversity of voices while seeking the best possible solution to the problem or answer to the question.

So what are the key characteristics of inquiry-based learning?
The following list will provide an important starting point in your thinking and planning for instruction.

- ☑ The teacher and/or students pose a question or a problem that is relevant to the students and the discipline.

- ☑ Posing this question or problem provokes students' wonder, curiosity, and speculation.

- ☑ The teacher models, scaffolds, and supports the stages of inquiry through ongoing assessment of student work.

- ☑ The teacher gradually releases responsibility for modelling as students gain more knowledge, skill, and confidence.

- ☑ To complete the inquiry meaningfully, the teacher and the students must have knowledge of major concepts and ideas within the discipline.

- ☑ To complete the inquiry successfully, the teacher and the students must have dispositions and attitudes that allow them to be curious, skeptical, empathetic, collaborative, and open to taking risks with their thinking.

- ☑ To complete the inquiry effectively, students must have problem-solving, critical thinking, collaborative, metacognitive, and communication skills.

Learning is a broad term that includes any gaining of new knowledge or skill. We learn through experience, practice, study, and other means. **Inquiry always begins with a wondering—a problem, a challenge, or a question.**

The origins of inquiry-based learning

Inquiry-based learning is rooted in progressive and constructivist educational and pedagogical philosophies. Its antecedents are found in the works of John Dewey, Lev Vygotsky, Paulo Freire, Howard Gardner, and others.

Progressive education

The progressive movement in education began in the late 19th century and continues to influence schooling to this day. One of the main beliefs of progressive education is that understanding is the result of social interaction. Social interactions help individual learners build knowledge. Progressive educators believe that in order to prepare students to engage more effectively in a democratic society, the classroom should model purposeful social interaction. Progressives also believe in "child-centred" classrooms where the diversity of learners is honoured through individualized instruction to meet the needs of all children. These beliefs are at odds with "traditional" or "rote" learning models of teaching where the teacher simply provides information and skill processes to the learner to memorize, recall, or perform.

Constructivism

Inquiry-based learning is also influenced by constructivism, a theory of learning developed in the early 20th century. Constructivists believe that humans construct reality through thinking. As a person matures, has new experiences, and engages in learning, his or her unique view of reality will expand, deepen, and become more sophisticated. Constructivist classrooms strive for rich and active learning environments that focus on real-world issues and contexts so that each learner can construct their own knowledge through experience. Learning is an active, social process that the teacher facilitates through a balance of structure and flexibility.

The beginnings of inquiry-based learning

Inquiry-based learning as a pedagogical method was first implemented in the 1960s in response to critiques of traditional forms of learning. The "space race" between the United States and the Soviet Union had triggered a renewed interest in educational techniques, especially in the science disciplines. New science curricula in the United States and other countries was developed with an inquiry focus in the belief that inquiry-based learning would lead to better learning and a competitive edge for students. In fact, research studies showed that the students in those first inquiry-based programs outperformed students in traditional classrooms (Shymansky *et al.*, 1990).

The debate on teaching strategies: Which is best?

You may have participated in conversations about which strategies should be used to improve student learning. Sometimes these discussions focus on the unhelpful question of "Which is best?" However, there is no definitive research evidence to suggest one universal best teaching practice.

A teacher's skill is found in his or her personal and professional ability to create a rich, inquiry-focused instructional program based on an understanding of how students learn best. This knowledge is achieved by accessing student prior knowledge and skills; developing a foundation of factual knowledge within the conceptual frameworks

THE ORIGINS OF INQUIRY-BASED LEARNING

Questioning traditional schooling

JOHN DEWEY (1859–1952) was an American pioneer in inquiry-based learning. As a former science teacher, Dewey felt that science teaching overly emphasized facts. He argued that teachers need to place more emphasis on science as a form of thinking and an attitude of mind. Dewey's inquiry model includes the following stages: presenting the problem, formulating a hypothesis, collecting data, and formulating a conclusion. In Dewey's model, as in all inquiry-based learning, the student is actively involved and the teacher is a skilled facilitator and guide. Dewey imagined the classroom as an interdependent community. Involvement in this community allows students to critically question truths through dialogue grounded in intellectual rigour.

PAULO FREIRE (1921–1997) was a Brazilian educational philosopher who claimed that schooling was based on a banking model: knowledge chosen by the teacher was placed into the passive learner's empty mind. Freire argued that this passive model should be replaced by a "critical pedagogy" of education as a political act that would transform the person and the world. Freire envisioned a form of education where men and women would free themselves from "oppressors" and "oppressive thinking." Freire, similar to Dewey, also emphasized dialogue as essential to learning and knowledge formation. Freire believed in active learning about real-world issues in social contexts. This belief resonates in inquiry-based learning today.

of a discipline; and by assessing each student's growing ability to think, problem solve, and work together.

A rich instructional program may include—in addition to inquiry-based learning—many different teaching practices, such as drill and practice, note-taking from lectures, inferring and critiquing text and images, using technology to communicate, and individual and group learning (see *Figure 1*).

Inquiry-based learning can be one of the most powerful teaching and learning strategies, but it does not exist in isolation from other strategies and, in fact, should be supported and sustained by them.

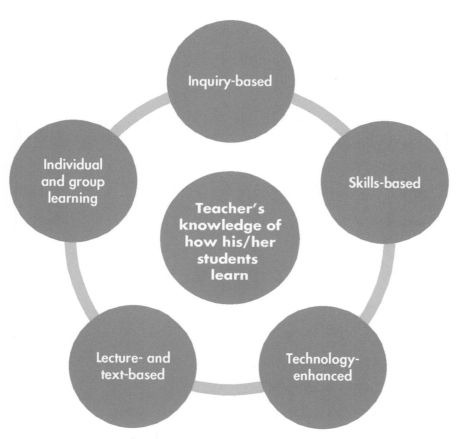

FIGURE 1: **Inquiry-based learning integrated with other strategies**

Why inquiry-based learning?

"We only think when confronted with a problem."

"Education is a social process; education is growth; education is not preparation for life but is life itself."

"Give the pupils something to do, not something to learn; and the doing is of such a nature as to demand thinking...; learning naturally results."

—John Dewey

"In problem-posing education, people develop their power to perceive critically the way they exist in the world with which and in which they find themselves; they come to see the world not as a static reality, but as a reality in process, in transformation.... Banking education resists dialogue; problem-posing education regards dialogue as indispensable to the act of cognition which unveils reality. Banking education treats students as objects of assistance; problem-posing education makes them critical thinkers."

—Paulo Freire, *Pedagogy of the Oppressed* (1970/2000)

Q What resonates with you in these quotes? What do you find problematic and why?

Q For which authentic problems about "life itself" could you could ask students to propose solutions?

Q How does Freire's belief in "problem-posing education" differ from traditional or "banking" education? In what ways do you consider yourself a problem-posing teacher? In what ways do you consider yourself a traditional teacher?

1.2 Why is inquiry-based learning effective?

Some educational researchers make a strong case for inquiry-based learning as a way to improve student learning. Inquiry-based learning became internationally famous through its formal implementation at McMaster University Medical School in the late 1960s (Neville, 2009).

Below is a snapshot of some of the key research that supports the positive effects of inquiry-based learning.

- An inquiry-based pedagogical approach has positive learning outcomes (Vajoczki *et al.*, 2011).

- Students are more likely to develop as engaged, self-directed learners in inquiry-based classrooms (Jang, Reeve, and Deci, 2010).

- Inquiry skill development leads to increases in critical thinking, the ability to undertake independent inquiry, and responsibility for students' own learning, intellectual growth, and maturity (Kuhn *et al.*, 2000).

- Present-day support for inquiry comes from cognitive science research that gives evidence of the importance of social activity and authentic contexts for learning (Greeno *et al.*, 1996).

- Inquiry-based classroom dialogue not only supports student academic learning but also supports social learning as students and teachers negotiate, share ideas, collaborate, and problem-solve together (Jennings and Mills, 2009).

- When investigating the effectiveness of inquiry-based learning using students' grades (in a university psychology course) as the outcome variable, results indicated that students who were taught using inquiry instruction had statistically significantly higher grades, when compared to their grades in the second semester of the course taught via traditional methods (Palmer, 2002).

Inquiry-based learning in the Information Age

Students today are consumers and producers of information. Digital technologies in particular allow them to be informed and entertained and to participate in social networks for different purposes. Our students' ability to use technologies in critical and creative ways to further their learning distinguishes them as 21st century learners.

Inquiry-based learning takes on a whole new dimension for students living in the Information Age. The teacher and the textbook are no longer the only expert sources of knowledge. When excited by learning, students can access multiple sources of information to satisfy their curiosity. The inquiry process can be individualized to meet students' interests and learning preferences, since students are no longer limited to traditional gathering of sources.

Of course, students need to hone their analytical skills when faced with so much information from so many sources. Teachers can respond to this need by modelling and facilitating the kind of analytical thinking required to conduct inquiry. They might also expect that the process and products of learning will not look the same as they once did. It is reasonable to expect that teachers will respond to students' considerable skill with digital technologies by encouraging their thoughtful, purposeful, and creative use—whether by encouraging Internet searches for evidence; collaborating on solving problems in a social network; or sharing ideas, conclusions, and questions with the wider digital world.

IQ: A Practical Guide to Inquiry-based Learning offers many practical suggestions for encouraging the use of digital technologies in the process and products of inquiry, and engaging students in authentic, problem-based learning.

> Our students' ability to use technologies in critical and creative ways to further their learning distinguishes them as 21st century learners.

Working through classroom inquiry with case studies

Whether you are new to inquiry-based learning or refining it as part of your current teaching practice, you may find it helpful to think about how it is used in different classroom situations. To that end, *IQ: A Practical Guide to Inquiry-based Learning* offers a number of instructive case studies.

In the following case study, begin by identifying the enablers and challenges to inquiry-based learning posed by the teacher. Consider whether your professional concerns are similar or dissimilar to hers.

Enablers and challenges to inquiry-based learning

Samir would like to begin adding some inquiry-based learning into her classroom practice, but doesn't know where to begin. She says she has "a set curriculum and texts and lessons that I've always relied on," but doesn't feel these materials "speak to kids today." She goes on:

> I'd really like to have kids more actively engaged in this course and thinking about important issues instead of merely covering massive amounts of content. I guess I'm also not sure how to teach the skills of inquiry other than having kids write research reports and essays. Also, how am I going to assess their work throughout the inquiry? It seems more complicated than marking homework and oral presentations.
>
> It would be great to work with some other teachers to bounce around some ideas of how this could work and what questions could become the focus of the course. I'm also a bit nervous that my kids can't handle a lot of self-directed work. I'm used to being the one in control. I guess I'm a bit traditional that way.

To help you delve into these questions, consider the research of Rachel Spronken-Smith *et al.* (2011), who identified the main enablers and challenges to the use of inquiry-based learning:

Enablers of inquiry-based learning	Challenges of inquiry-based learning
Student-centred teaching philosophy	Difficulty of teaching inquiry for the first time
Course design with open-ended questions, collaborative learning, active engagement, and scaffolding of required inquiry skills	Time needed for inquiry-based learning activities (often more time than "traditional" teaching methods)
Resources about inquiry-based learning to support the teacher	Coping with varied assessment products
School culture and institutional norms that encourage the use of inquiry	Providing students with opportunities to learn and practise self-reflection and self-evaluation

FIGURE 2: **Enablers and challenges of inquiry-based learning**

Q What do you infer are the main enablers and challenges for Samir?

Q Do any of Samir's concerns resonate with you? Why?

Q Considering the list in *Figure 2*, what do you see as your main challenges?

Q What do you see as your main enablers in the implementation of inquiry-based learning?

Q What supports do you require and how will you advocate for them?

1.3

What are various types of inquiry?

Inquiry-based learning is not meant to be prescriptive for the teacher or the student; it is an interactive, fluid, and recursive process responsive to the discipline, the teaching goals, and student learning needs. While the fundamental characteristics of inquiry do not change, there are different types of inquiry that may be best suited to different situations, depending on the question or problem posed and the needs of students.

Variations of inquiry: open, guided, blended

At one end of the continuum of student choice is an **open** inquiry. This is an inquiry where students choose the question and design and conduct the investigation independently. Obviously, students must be highly skilled and experienced in inquiry in order to undertake this type of inquiry.

At the opposite end of the continuum is **guided** inquiry where you assist throughout the process, by selecting the question, providing specific frameworks and resources in the investigation, and modelling the critical analysis required of the accrued research. Teachers in guided inquiry also preselect the way in which students articulate their new understandings—perhaps through written work, oral presentations, or multimedia creations. This type of inquiry is the best for students (and teachers) who are just beginning to learn the required skills needed to complete an inquiry.

A **blended** inquiry represents all the possibilities in the middle of the continuum between "open" and "guided." This is where both open and guided inquiry co-exist. You decide when and where to give student autonomy and where you need to step in to explicitly teach the required skills. Blended inquiry is the form of inquiry most often attempted in classrooms since it allows for balance and flexibility in teacher and student direction.

> Inquiry-based learning is an interactive, fluid, and recursive process responsive to the discipline, the teaching goals, and student learning needs.

The chart below details the different degrees of student autonomy within the essential features of an inquiry.

MORE STUDENT AUTONOMY → → → MORE TEACHER DIRECTION				
Learner engages in discipline-oriented questions	Poses a question	Selects among questions, poses new questions	Sharpens or clarifies questions provided by teacher, materials, or other sources	Engages in questions provided by teacher, materials, or other sources
Learner gives priority to evidence in responding to questions	Determines what constitutes evidence and collects evidence	Directed to collect certain evidence	Given evidence and asked to analyze	Given evidence and told how to analyze
Learner formulates explanations from evidence	Formulates explanation after summarizing evidence	Guided in process of formulating explanations from evidence	Given possible ways to use evidence to formulate explanation	Provided with evidence
Learner connects explanations to discipline knowledge	Independently examines other resources and forms the links to explanations	Directed toward areas and sources of discipline knowledge	Learner given possible connections	
Learner communicates and justifies explanation	Forms reasonable and logical argument to communicate explanations	Coached in development of communication	Learner provided broad guidelines to sharpen communication	Learner given steps and procedures for communication

FIGURE 3: **Features of inquiry and variations of student autonomy**

Source: Reprinted with permission from *Inquiry and the National Science Education Standards.* Copyright 2000 by the National Academies of Sciences. Courtesy of the National Academy Press, Washington, D.C.

Alone or together?

You may choose to have students work on an investigation independently, with partners, or in groups. Groups may be formed by assigning students according to their demonstrated ability to complete a successful inquiry. Keep in mind that one of the fundamental qualities of inquiry is that students work together to make sense of a question or problem as part of a democratic community of learners.

How do I ensure that I begin with a good inquiry question that excites my students and focuses on the big ideas of my discipline?

Good question!

As teachers, we are always trying to improve our ability to formulate good questions that will make students want to think.

Here are a few points to consider when creating good questions with students:

A good question...

- ☑ is an invitation to think (not recall, summarize, or detail)

- ☑ comes from genuine curiosity and confusion about the world

- ☑ makes you think about something in a way you never considered before

- ☑ invites both deep thinking and deep feelings; leads to more good questions

- ☑ asks you to think critically, creatively, ethically, productively, and reflectively about essential ideas in a discipline

SOURCE: Adapted from Barell, John, *Developing More Curious Minds*, ASCD (2003).

Here are examples of a few questions that could launch an inquiry process:

- ■ Is Canada a good country?

- ■ Is illegal action ever justified when trying to cause political change?

- ■ What will Canadian communities look like in the future?

ENSURING SUCCESS

How do you know where to start when creating an inquiry question?

Curriculum documents and other key resources that clearly identify big ideas, major concepts, and fundamental questions are a good place to start when planning an inquiry.

There is no reason to "reinvent the wheel"—many discipline experts have grappled with articulating the most fundamental ideas and crucial questions of a discipline, so feel confident if you start with this best thinking. Collaborating with colleagues in this planning stage allows you to share your ideas and anticipate challenges students may face.

REVISIT AND REFLECT

This introductory chapter outlined inquiry-based learning in broad strokes. It considered its historical and philosophical roots in education, and the research—both past and present—that supports inquiry as a way to engage learners in constructing knowledge and solving problems. It presented opportunities to reflect on some of the enabling conditions and challenges of inquiry-based learning in your classroom. Finally, the main types of inquiry were distinguished with respect to student autonomy.

At the end of the chapter, you had the opportunity to think about how to begin planning for an inquiry-based unit of study. In the next chapter, you will begin to think more specifically about planning for assessment of inquiry-based learning with the following guiding principle in mind:

It is important to **accurately** *and* **continually** *assess students' learning throughout an inquiry process to determine the degree of guidance, scaffolding, and modelling required.*

To conclude your exploration of this chapter, take some time to think through these questions:

Q Why are you interested in inquiry-based learning?

Q What degree of autonomy during the inquiry process do you think would best work with your students—open, guided, or blended?

Q From what you've read so far, why do you think inquiry-based learning is important in the Information Age?

Q Describe your greatest challenge when it comes to implementing inquiry-based learning. What ideas from this chapter could help you overcome this challenge?

CHAPTER 2
ASSESSMENT OF
INQUIRY

2.1

How do I gather valid evidence of learning during an inquiry?

At this point, you have done some initial thinking about the potential of engaging students with inquiry-based learning. The inquiry process allows for a variety of important types of thinking. It demands that students are curious and ask relevant and provocative questions with a disciplinary focus. It also demands critical and creative thinking skills in evaluating sources, proposing solutions, and examining multiple perspectives. In order to evaluate student learning, teachers must find sources of evidence, such as written and oral communication.

This chapter examines how student learning can be made visible throughout an inquiry for the purpose of assessment. Suggestions are offered on how to assess the skills of inquiry and critical thinking, and how to make tangible the dispositions students need to persevere and grow as learners. It should be stressed that your own efforts to create an inquiry-friendly classroom climate will also help to ensure valid assessments.

What is assessment?

Assessment is evidence that we gather of student learning. The purpose of assessment is to help students to improve in their learning. Assessment also provides critical information to you on how to best support students to further their learning.

Think of a typical day in your class: you are continually assessing students in multiple ways. You may be checking their facial expressions for agreement, boredom, or perplexity. You may be listening to their answers and noting if their thinking is logical or muddled. Or you may be observing them at work in collaborative groups, asking each other questions and puzzling over an issue together. It is at these moments that you have the opportunity to collect assessment data that will inform the next steps in teaching. Student voice provides one of the richest ways to accurately determine what a student is thinking. Written reflections by students are another valuable source of assessment data.

This chapter examines how student learning can be made visible throughout an inquiry for the purpose of assessment.

In order to collect reliable and valid evidence of learning during an inquiry, you can intentionally triangulate the data that you collect while considering the feedback you will give that will provide the next steps for student learning. The ideas of triangulation of data and the importance of feedback are used throughout this chapter and the chapters to follow.

The three areas of triangulation are conversations, observations, and products.

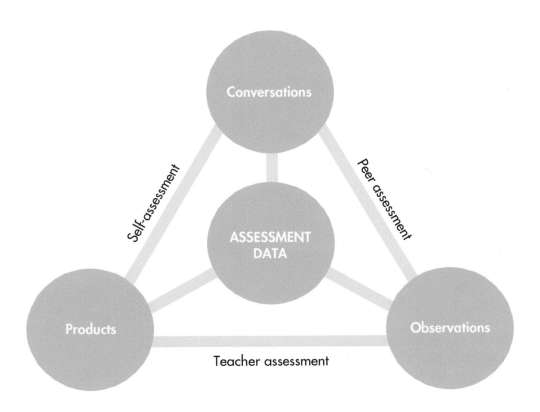

FIGURE 4: **Triangulation of assessment data**

Conversations

Conversations are moments when students reveal their thinking to their teachers and to each other. During conversations, participants try to make sense of the other person's thinking in many different ways, such as formal questioning during class discussions and informal questioning during collaborative work. Listening carefully to students' voices will help you consider what understanding the student is demonstrating at all stages of problem solving and inquiry. Teachers and students also engage in conversations to help students clarify, extend, and defend their thinking.

A student is busy gathering and assessing sources. You start a conversation with him based on the following question:

You: *How do you know this is reliable information?*

His answers may reveal both his abilities and frustrations in assessing sources:

Student: *This is a government website so I guess it is totally from their point of view. I can't find any information about this blog author but I like what she has to say.*

Now you have the chance to provide immediate feedback that can move his thinking forward:

You: *You are right to say the government website reveals their point of view. Where else could you go to get another perspective?*

You also have the chance to address his challenges:

You: *Why do you think it is important to know the blog author's credibility and point of view? What other sources do you have?*

(NOTE: Chapter 3 elaborates on questioning for students and teachers.)

Observations

Observations occur when you attend carefully to students with specific learning goals and criteria in mind. We can observe a student taking notes, summarizing text, making a presentation, and collaborating with their peers. As we observe, we are intentional in what we are looking for—for example, clarity, accuracy, critical thinking, or collaborative skills such as taking turns and listening to others respectfully. Written records of observations help us recall where the student is in his or her learning and help us think about explicit feedback to give to the student.

For example, if we note during collaborative group work that a student does not use many criteria when assessing a source ("I found it on the web; therefore, it must be true"), then we can return to that student and ask them to consider what criteria to look for in a web resource. (Who created it? For what purpose? How do you know it is truthful? What position is taken and what arguments are made?)

Here's another example. Let's say you have asked students to assess a partner's inquiry questions based on the following criteria: 1) the question must be open-ended, i.e., have no definitive answer;

2) be relevant to the topics and big ideas being studied; and
3) involve an important problem that involves thinking and feeling. As you observe the students discussing their questions—"What is climate change?" and "What are the results of climate change to our environment?"—you note that the students are only considering the criteria of relevance to unit topics and are missing the other two criteria. If the students conclude that their questions are good inquiry questions, you will know that the students need more practice with creating such questions, especially how to move from single-answer content questions to complex, multiple-perspective questions. You may also choose to pose questions to make students aware of the other criteria in order to nudge their thinking: "Can you find the answer to this question in our textbook?" or "Does this question require that you find different perspectives and draw a conclusion?"

Conversations and observations are intended as types of assessment that inform the teacher and the student when, where, and why thinking gets stuck and how best to move along.

Products

Products tend to be more formal pieces of assessment data. These are data that you have structured to take a snapshot of the student's ability at a certain point in time. Products enable you to assess a number of skills and/or a cluster of curriculum expectations and goals. Products are diverse, ranging from the written solution to a mathematics problem to an oral presentation on an environmental issue.

By increasing your assessment repertoire beyond a single source of evidence (e.g., products), and by using triangulated assessment data, you can be more confident of the validity of your assessment. Why? Because students may reveal their understanding and demonstrate their learning at times and in ways that are not always revealed in formal products. Think of the student who "freezes" during a test or doesn't perform to his or her potential in an end-of-unit evaluation. That performance may not be a valid or reliable indicator of what the student truly knows or is capable of doing. For this reason, you should feel empowered to look to other sources of evidence that you have collected. Conversations, observations, and a variety of products are not only good for assessing learners, they allow you to check in on learning in order to inform your own practice and adjust what and how you are teaching accordingly.

Assessment impacts instruction

It is important to accurately and continually assess students' learning throughout an inquiry process to determine the degree of guidance, scaffolding, and modelling required. Use the reproducibles provided in this book to record evidence of learning for each student.

2.2 How do I model and assess growth of inquiry dispositions?

Before examining some practical ideas on assessing an inquiry, it is important to step back and consider the classroom conditions that foster curiosity and inquiry-based thinking in students and help make learning meaningful and engaging.

Inquiry-based learning can only succeed when a caring, cooperative, and curious classroom culture is established, modelled, and promoted. Some of the most vital aspects of this culture include:

- high academic and behavioural expectations,
- student voice and choice,
- positive peer interactions, and
- effective feedback.

So, how do you put curiosity at the forefront of your classroom? One way to encourage curiosity is to learn more about your students' lives and interests. Take time, especially in the beginning of a course, to allow all learners to thoughtfully consider the diversity of experiences, personalities, and knowledge in the room. Modelling and demanding respect for all learners is very important. Students will not take risks if they think they will "lose face" for being wrong. Make sure that during discussions, students listen to each other and not just to you. You can do this by asking students to paraphrase, ask questions, or to make connections to what the previous speaker has said.

Devote time to talking about why hearing multiple perspectives and working with people with diverse skills and interests leads to deeper learning for all. Asking questions such as, "Why do you think it is important to consider different points of view on issues?" and, "Do you think that working with others helps you learn in different ways?" helps students reflect if they are being curious, flexible, and open-minded learners. Presenting students with controversial issues from a one-sided

> Inquiry-based learning can only succeed when a caring, cooperative, and curious classroom culture is established, modelled, and promoted.

perspective and then gradually introducing different perspectives also helps them to see how their initial thinking can be challenged, adapted, and strengthened, and why single perspectives can be superficial, inadequate, and/or misleading.

Certain habits or dispositions can also be encouraged and practised during inquiry-based learning. These habits include curiosity, self confidence in one's ability to reason, flexibility in thinking, open-mindedness, perseverance, taking reasonable risks, and reflection. This list of learner dispositions is not exhaustive and you (or your board or district) may have certain qualities that you feel are important to cultivate in your students. Refer to *Reproducible 1: How to Model and Assess Inquiry Dispositions* on pp. 136–137 to talk about the importance of inquiry dispositions with your students, to assess these dispositions, and to provide a self-reflection tool for students.

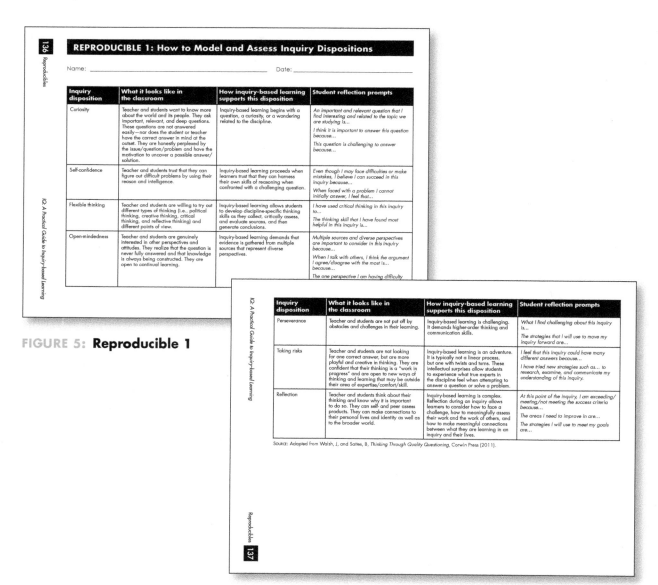

FIGURE 5: **Reproducible 1**

2.3

Where and how do I begin planning for an inquiry with a focus on assessment?

So far, you've explored the foundational qualities of inquiry and the classroom conditions needed to foster students' inquiry thinking. Now it is time for you to create a concrete plan. Your decisions will be informed by your students' learning needs and where you are in your teaching program.

When planning inquiry-based learning, start by gathering board and Ministry documents that articulate curriculum goals, expectations, and grade standards. These resources clearly define key ideas and questions in addition to core concepts and skills that are important to the discipline. Some of these documents might even suggest inquiry questions to consider. They may also provide important information on how to assess evidence of student learning through the process and product stages.

Your goal is to have students design and conduct a successful inquiry and to communicate the results. Consider *Reproducible 2: Inquiry Rubric* on p. 138 as a framework for both assessing and evaluating the evidence of student success in the inquiry and as a starting point for co-constructing specific success criteria with students. Co-constructing success criteria for the final product and for the inquiry processes allows students to take ownership of their learning and to assess their own progress. If this is the first inquiry, you may want to model some of the important criteria. As successive inquiries are undertaken, students should be asked to refine the criteria as their understanding of what makes a successful inquiry deepens.

Co-constructing success criteria for the final product and for the inquiry processes allows students to take ownership of their learning and to assess their own progress.

REPRODUCIBLE 2: Inquiry Rubric

Name: _____ Date: _____

Goal: To design and conduct a successful inquiry and to communicate the results.

Curriculum Expectations:_____

Final Product: _____

Success Criteria Categories*	High degree of effectiveness	Considerable effectiveness	Some effectiveness	Limited effectiveness	Further support required
Inquiry skills and processes **The student will** ask and refine relevant questions that further the investigation gather and analyze multiple sources critically evaluate evidence and make valid conclusions					
Application of thinking skills in proposing a course of action **The student will** transfer critical, creative, and discipline-based thinking skills when proposing an answer to the inquiry question or proposing a course of practical action					
Communicate new understandings **The student will** communicate clearly communicate persuasively engage the audience use the vocabulary and terminology of the discipline					
Learn what is currently known about the topic/problem **The student will** demonstrate knowledge and understanding of content important to the inquiry					

*Success Criteria: Success criteria should be co-constructed between teacher and student as appropriate. Success criteria answer the question "What are the specific characteristics of a successful inquiry?"

FIGURE 6: **Reproducible 2**

Reproducible 2: Inquiry Rubric balances the process skills required of an investigation with the final product. Through conversations, observations, and products, you determine how students are succeeding in the following four categories:

- Inquiry skills and processes
- Application of thinking skills in proposing a course of action
- Communicating new understandings
- Learning what is currently known about the topic/problem

Your choice of a final product allows students to share their new understanding with a community of learners. The product needs to be suited to your students, the learning goals, and an intended audience and purpose. A final product should be announced at the beginning of the inquiry and should be motivational and engaging in order to propel the inquiry. Products could include position papers, public service announcements, poster displays, exhibits, photo essays, and multimedia products such as blogs, wikis, or video diaries, just to name a few.

As important as the final product is to assess and evaluate, keep in mind that the emphasis for gathering evidence of student learning cannot be solely on final products. Overemphasis on the product may devalue the essential experiences of the process of inquiry.

CASE STUDY

Co-constructing success criteria for an inquiry

Daniel wants to co-construct the success criteria for an inquiry with his students so they understand what is expected from them during the process and for a final product. This is the first time his students are engaged in a guided inquiry so he realizes that in order to arrive at the success criteria, he must have some criteria in his "back pocket" to guide the students. The fundamental criteria that Daniel has in mind are framed in student-friendly language:

☑ I understand the knowledge and information important to the inquiry and the discipline.

☑ I have developed relevant, rich questions to guide my inquiry.

☑ I have gathered and analyzed information from a variety of sources and perspectives.

☑ I understand the main ideas, arguments, and positions represented in the sources and can clearly explain them.

☑ I understand the limitations of sources and how other perspectives may be missing and sought more information when needed.

☑ I have developed, chosen, and used relevant criteria in order to successfully answer the inquiry question.

☑ I have enough information to answer the inquiry question.

Daniel shows his students a visual representation of the inquiry process (see *Figure 7*). He asks them to think about what each step of the inquiry process means by first using a relevant real-life example of a practical inquiry that involves making a decision:

You are thinking about buying a new laptop computer. How will you decide which is best? What questions will you ask and of whom? What information will you gather? How will you make a judgment?

continued

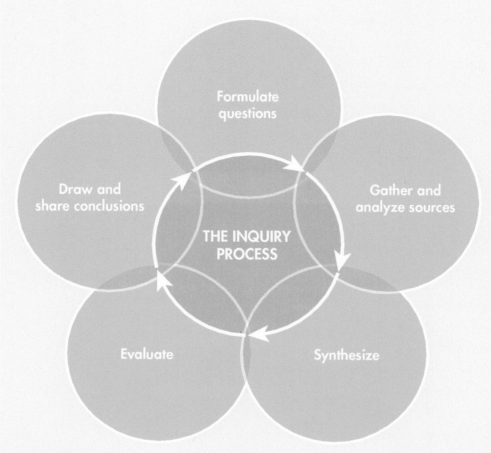

FIGURE 7: **The inquiry process**

Students share their answers, and Daniel highlights how their answers fit into the inquiry process visual. For example, Daniel responds to a student who says, "I'd ask my friend who is a techie for her opinion" by showing how this is called "analyzing a source"—a friend is a source and the student's rationale for selecting this "source" is due to her known expertise. To another student who says that he would ask the question "How long is the laptop going to last?" Daniel replies that this question is a good example of "formulating questions" (the durability of the laptop) to make a judgment. Daniel realizes that students must become familiar and comfortable with the language of inquiry in order to clearly articulate their thinking during the assessment and to further their abilities.

Daniel also outlines how each stage of inquiry must be carefully completed and lead to a supported answer, as opposed to being incomplete and leading to an unsupported answer.

Complete and supported answer

I chose the laptop after asking questions of salespeople, friends, and reading articles online comparing brands and environmental impacts. I analyzed the pros and cons of many laptops and had criteria to make my choice—price and durability.

Incomplete and unsupported answer

I chose the laptop my friend got because it seemed to work for her. I never asked about battery life, warranty cost, or consumer reports. I did ask about the laptop colour.

Daniel asks his students to elaborate on what makes a "successful" inquiry versus an "unsuccessful" inquiry. He then poses another deeper, discipline-related question, one that the students are familiar with, and repeats the process of considering the stages of a successful inquiry. The question is "How do we know what we know about history?"

Finally, he returns to the visual of the inquiry process and asks students to generate one or two specific criteria for a successful inquiry using the following headings:

- Posing a question
- Understanding what is already known
- Gathering evidence
- Proposing a solution and communicating new understandings

He refines their responses as needed by asking extending and clarifying questions. His students begin to see that an inquiry is anchored in an open question, that it demands that they think deeply, research effectively, and respond clearly and persuasively. He posts this preliminary version of inquiry success criteria. The chart is consulted throughout the inquiry and the criteria are extended and refined as needed. The chart becomes an important anchor in the classroom and students refer to it often as a means of peer and self-assessment. They begin to see themselves as inquiry learners and can use the vocabulary of inquiry correctly and effectively. As the inquiry progresses, Daniel and his students showcase work that exemplifies quality thinking in each stage of the inquiry process.

Q Discuss the potential benefits of Daniel's approach to co-constructing the assessment of an inquiry with his students.

Q Consider the challenges to implementing a similar approach in your classroom. How might you modify this approach to best meet the needs of your students?

Inquiry is iterative

Although inquiry has been presented in sequential stages or steps, it is not a linear process. Inquiry is an interactive, iterative, and fluid process responsive to the discipline, teaching goals, and student learning needs.

You'll probably note this fluidity when students are working critically with evidence and creating arguments and explanations. It is at this point that the steps mesh together and students will fold back to revise the inquiry question, rethink the evidence, and consider the explanation from different viewpoints. Be prepared for the messiness that naturally arises from a critical and creative inquiry project. It is as a result of these processes that deep learning occurs for your students.

The four domains of inquiry assessment

Note that *Reproducible 2: Inquiry Rubric* proposes four general domains within which students demonstrate their knowledge, understanding, and skill. The first domain is **inquiry skills and processes**. These are the foundational skills that are crucial for a student to attain in order to become an efficient and successful inquiry thinker. To assess inquiry skills and processes, you could use specific criteria such as the student's ability to ask and refine relevant questions to further an investigation, the student's ability to gather and analyze multiple sources critically, and the student's skill at evaluating sources and making a valid conclusion based on the sources.

The second domain of inquiry assessment is the student's **application of critical, creative, and disciplinary thinking** (such as mathematical, political, and geographical thinking) in assessing evidence and in proposing a course of action in response to the inquiry question.

In the third domain, students are assessed on their ability to **communicate their new understandings**. The final domain of inquiry assessment is based on student's **knowledge and understanding** of what is currently known about the topic and/or problem.

To simplify, the four domains of inquiry assessment involve inquiry process skills, application of these skills, communication, and demonstration of fundamental knowledge related to the inquiry. These four domains are similar to achievement chart categories in many curriculum documents.

For each of the four domains, you could create a planning template that outlines the products, observations, and conversations (triangulation of data) that you may use as valid evidence of student learning. A planning template will let you and your students see the "big picture" of learning goals and how they will be assessed. A planning template allows you to figure out what students already know, what they need to know, and how you are going to help them move their learning forward.

A filled-in sample of a planning template is provided on the next page as *Figure 8: Inquiry assessment planning example*. The template includes the four inquiry assessment domains; specific criteria within the domains; and suggestions for observations, conversations, and products that could be used to determine if students are moving forward in their learning (a blank template is provided as *Reproducible 3: Inquiry Assessment Planning Template* on p. 139). The conversation prompts provided can be used informally to speak with selected students while the class is working on collaborative or independent tasks, or in more formal conferencing with students. For both observations and conversations, it makes sense to document the data in a way that you are comfortable with (e.g., using a tablet computer, written records, video/audio recordings). Please note that the sample planning template in *Figure 8* provides suggestions only. You are the expert in your classroom and must decide on the best assessment data to inform your students' learning and your teaching practice.

Each suggested product, observation, and conversation may need to be repeated until students are successful in demonstrating their learning. If your triangulated evidence reveals that students have mastered a particular skill or demonstrated their understanding of knowledge, then you can be confident in proceeding with the inquiry and/or allowing greater student autonomy. The planning template outlines assessment evidence, but many of the examples provided could become evaluation data used to judge if students are reaching the learning goals.

Evaluations should occur at the end of a series of learning opportunities, after students have received instruction and have had independent opportunities to practise and perfect the skills required for a task. Evaluations can be oral presentations, essays, or tests.

Q&A

What is the difference between assessment and evaluation?

Assessment occurs through the process of learning in order to provide the teacher with information about student progress and to trigger feedback to enhance that progress. Assessments also tell you how to adjust your teaching. If the assessment reveals that students already know the skill, you would provide them opportunities to apply the skill. If the assessment reveals that many students are still developing a skill, you would provide them with practice and constructive feedback. If the assessment reveals that hardly any students have proficiency in a skill, then the skill must be re-taught in an intentional manner.

Evaluation occurs at the end of a cycle of learning opportunities where the teacher must make an informed professional judgment about the quality of the student's learning.

Inquiry Domains: What a student needs to know and do during an inquiry	Ways to gather evidence of student learning		
	Products	Observations	Conversations
Inquiry skills and processes			
Student asks and refines relevant questions that further the investigation.	Student identifies good inquiry questions from a list of options and provides a written explanation of choice.	Observe student ranking various questions you have provided from deepest to superficial.	What makes a good inquiry question?
			How does this question link to important concepts we have discussed?
	Student creates a flow chart of initial questions to final revised question.	Observe student peer assess questions.	How could you improve this question?
		Observe student creating questions based on provocative quotes, photographs, statistical data, etc., that you have provided.	
Student gathers and analyzes multiple sources critically.	Student provides a brief written analysis of teacher-selected online, written, statistical, and oral sources.	Observe student brainstorming what sources she or he thinks would be most useful in their research and explaining why to their peers.	How do you identify credible sources?
			What kinds of sources should you use?
	Student analyzes bibliographies provided by the teacher to determine credibility and point of view and makes group presentation of findings.	Observe student in the library and/or on the Internet collecting and making choices regarding sources of evidence.	How do you know this is reliable information?
	Student asked to assess the credibility of chosen sources in an annotated bibliography.		
Student evaluates evidence and makes a valid conclusion.	Student identifies bias, point of view, and missing perspectives from teacher-selected sources in a written paragraph.	Observe student collaborating to evaluate one piece of evidence and ask her or him to make a preliminary conclusion. The student then participates in a jigsaw with other groups who have been given different sources of evidence and have drawn different conclusions.	What is the evidence suggesting to you?
			Are you missing any perspectives?
	Student draws conclusions based on evidence in written report.		Have you gathered enough evidence to answer the question?
			Does your conclusion make sense considering your evidence?

	Products / Evidence	Observations	Questions
Application of thinking skills in proposing a course of action Student transfers critical, creative, and disciplinary thinking skills when proposing a course of practical action.	Student proposes a course of practical action in an oral presentation or written report in response to an inquiry question. Student debates different courses of action. Student creates social media that reflects their course of action.	Observe student discussing various courses of action in response to the inquiry question. Observe student trying to convince others of the merits of their proposed course of action. Observe student getting advice and feedback from peers on their proposed course of action.	What thinking skills helped you arrive at this course of action? How did you reconsider or revise your own thinking? Why do you think this course of action is the best? How do you think you are becoming better at conducting inquiries?
Communicates new understandings Student communicates clearly. Student communicates persuasively. Student engages the audience. Student uses the vocabulary and terminology of the discipline.	Oral presentations Conference panels Written essay Presentation of new understanding using ICT (e.g., blog, wiki) Written assessments	Observe student during collaborative work. Observe student during peer assessments. Observe student when she/he is asked to create a key visual to aid them in completing a writing task. Observe student during rehearsal stages for oral presentation.	Can you summarize your main points for me? In what ways could you improve your written/oral language? How could you communicate in a more interesting and engaging way? Who is the audience? What strategies could you use to be a better writer/speaker?
Learns what is currently known about the topic/problem Student demonstrates knowledge and understanding of content important to the inquiry.	Quiz/test questions Posters Key visuals Models Written and oral responses	Observe student in the library and/or using the Internet to collect and make choices regarding sources of evidence. Observe student's ability to grasp foundational knowledge during class discussions and collaborative group work.	Can you define X in your own words? Can you tell me the significance of X? Can you give me an example of X? Why is this similar to X? How is it different?

FIGURE 8: Inquiry assessment planning example

2.4 How can feedback raise student achievement?

Now that you have gathered evidence of student learning, how can you provide effective feedback that will give students the opportunity to improve during the inquiry?

Recent education research by John Hattie (2008), Dylan Wiliam (2011), and Grant Wiggins (2012) has focused on the importance of formative assessment in increasing student learning and achievement. Research has shown that one crucial strategy of formative assessment, providing effective feedback, leads to higher achievement—when accepted and acted on by the learner.

Giving feedback is a sophisticated skill. Feedback is not advice or praise, or highlighting mistakes or deficiencies to the learner. Feedback must be specific to the learning goal, and helpful to the learner in that "actionable" information is provided. Feedback makes the learner think and must be offered in a supportive and timely fashion. Contrary to our best intentions, our feedback is often misunderstood or rejected and does not motivate students in the long term.

To illustrate, let's say that a student in your class has just generated a list of possible inquiry questions. Her questions are low-level and can be answered by a factual search. Consider the various possible statements that you could offer to the student, and think about which one of these four statements is actually feedback in its truest sense:

1. I know you can do better than these. Try to think more deeply.
2. Are you really trying your best to develop thoughtful questions?
3. Take a look at Jill's questions and tell me how yours differ.
4. This question does not ask you to think deeply. Do you know of a problem or challenge within your topic that interests you and would require you to investigate many points of view and consider different opinions before reaching an answer?

> Feedback must be specific to the learning goal, and helpful to the learner in that "actionable" information is provided.

If you selected the fourth statement, you are correct. This statement is relatively easy to identify because it has a degree of specificity that the other statements lack. However, we know that instead of providing actual feedback, we sometimes give praise to students (statement 1); try to offer motivation that does little to improve learning (statement 2); or provide advice that may not prove helpful and/or may impede the student's motivation (statement 3).

The key to skilfully providing feedback to students is knowledge of the criteria for success and the ability to define those criteria in a way that is clear, stimulates student thinking, and doesn't shut students down. Skilfully articulating to students what makes a good question, what makes a good source, or what a logical conclusion

The importance of feedback

"Although the universal teacher lament that there's no time for such feedback is understandable, remember that "no time to give and use feedback" actually means "no time to cause learning." As we have seen, research shows that less teaching plus more feedback is the key to achieving greater learning. And there are numerous ways—through technology, peers, and other teachers—that students can get the feedback they need. So try it out. Less teaching, more feedback."

—Grant Wiggins, "Seven keys to effective feedback" (2012)

"If we are to harness the power of feedback to increase student learning, then we need to ensure that feedback causes a cognitive rather than an emotional reaction—in other words, feedback should cause thinking. It should be focused; it should relate to the learning goals that have been shared with the students; and it should be more work for the recipient than the donor. Indeed, the whole purpose of feedback should be to increase the extent to which students are owners of their own learning...."

—Dylan Wiliam, *Embedded Formative Assessment* (2011)

Q Consider the positions of Wiggins and Wiliam. How do their beliefs resonate with you? How do they support or challenge your practice and how might you meet any challenges in order to provide more effective feedback to your students?

looks like before students are asked to apply this knowledge is key, since a shared understanding allows for improvement to occur in a strategic way.

The other important feature about feedback is that the teacher is not the only one responsible for providing it. Peers can provide feedback to each other. The most important feedback, of course, comes from learners thinking through the quality of their own work. Make time in your class to explicitly model and teach the qualities of giving and receiving feedback. The remaining chapters of the book will provide suggestions on ways to promote the use of feedback with your students in order to make them more autonomous learners.

Evaluation and reporting

If you think about the sophisticated learning that occurs during an inquiry, it is difficult to "boil it down" to a final mark for reporting purposes. The basic question of reporting that must be answered through your professional judgment is, "To what degree did the student achieve the learning goals?" The following guidelines are designed to help you with these reporting decisions.

Your school or board policies may outline what percent of a mark in a course comprises a final evaluation of performance tasks and what percent of a mark in a course comprises evaluations throughout the course. Let's say, for example, that the final evaluation in a course is 25% and the other evaluations are 75%. Since you will need to weigh the evaluations throughout the course in terms of their importance, it makes sense to attempt to balance them in some way. Perhaps you have planned for your students to conduct four inquiries throughout the course. You may decide that the final evaluations for each inquiry involve some type of written and oral communication product that are weighed equally.

We have suggested gathering your assessment and evaluation data in four domains that could also be equally weighed: inquiry skills and processes, applying inquiry skills, communicating new understandings, and demonstrating knowledge of content important to the inquiry. So in the four inquiries, students would be assessed and evaluated in four domains.

Now comes more professional judgment. Again you must decide how to weigh the evidence in the four inquiries. You may also decide that the evaluations for the first inquiry in the course be weighed less

> The most important feedback comes from learners thinking through the quality of their own work.

than the ones at the end since students should progress and improve with additional practice. Or you may decide they should be weighed equally since you will be providing less directed instruction and more student autonomy throughout each inquiry. The fact of the matter is that you can get lost in marks sheets and software that may give you a false sense of fairness in reporting. Reporting is an interpretive event but one that demands thoughtful and equitable processes.

We would stress that an inquiry in itself is a rich performance task that should carry greater weight than other evidence since it reveals more about the student's knowledge and skills. The final choice of a report card mark asks you to consider which evidence is most important and how well the student achieved overall, while carefully attending to the most recent evidence in particular.

We would encourage you to develop a common understanding with your colleagues on the process for determining a final grade in addition to communicating this process to your students.

REVISIT AND REFLECT

Assessment and inquiry instruction were braided together in this chapter. Two assumptions of the chapter were that:

- assessment improves both teaching and learning, and
- inquiry is a dynamic process where learners assess themselves and each other.

The fact that all learners can recognize and respond to the learning *while it is taking place* during an inquiry is what inquiry assessment is all about.

Some techniques to increase learners' recognition of and response to inquiry-based learning were provided: sharing learning goals; co-constructing success criteria; gathering evidence from conversations, observations, and products; and providing effective feedback. Some planning tools were offered to aid you in implementing these techniques.

It was also stressed that developing a classroom culture of curiosity is important to maximize learning and to allow valid assessments and evaluations to occur. The dispositions of an inquiry thinker—curiosity, self confidence in one's own ability to reason, flexibility in thinking, open-mindedness, perseverance, taking reasonable risks, and reflection—are dispositions that will carry our students (and ourselves as teachers) beyond the classroom walls and into our communities as thoughtful, caring citizens.

To conclude your exploration of this chapter, take some time to think through these questions:

Q How do you gather assessment evidence from your students? Do you feel you have balanced evidence from triangulated sources? How would you address an imbalance, if there is one?

Q How does the idea of inquiry dispositions resonate with you? How could you engage your students in thinking about how and why inquiry dispositions affect their learning?

Q What are some specific ways you could explicitly model giving feedback and receiving feedback on an inquiry task?

Q How are you envisioning inquiry-based learning in your class and how do you plan to assess it?

CHAPTER 3
FORMULATE
QUESTIONS

Why bother creating inquiry questions?

Learning begins with a question. Questions arise from our daily puzzlements about how the world works, why people act in a certain way, or whether what we know is true. Questions are the fuel we need to help us develop as thinkers.

So, what is the role of education in creating inquisitive minds? In a major sense, it is to pose the right questions. Students who are asked ethical questions are more likely to grow as ethical thinkers. Students who are asked geographical questions are more likely to grow as geographical thinkers. Students who are asked questions related to human systems and institutions are more likely to grow as historical and political thinkers. As students improve at different types of questioning and thinking, they become better prepared to fulfill their potential as "thinking" citizens of a complex world. As curious citizens, they may be more inclined to question what is, to draw conclusions about what could and should be, and to act upon their thinking.

Our job as teachers is to model good questioning skills and to create opportunities for students to ask and answer interesting and powerful questions arising from course content. Not only do we want students to develop proficiency in asking thoughtful and relevant discipline-related questions, we want them to ask the *right kind of questions* during the inquiry process. In this chapter, we'll offer examples of both discipline-based inquiry questions that develop disciplinary thinking, and analytical questions that develop reasoning and self-reflective thinking.

Nurturing curiosity in all our learners can be a challenge, especially when we detect a high level of reluctance or "disengagement." Students, as well as teachers, may need to "unlearn" previous habits such as memorizing content as the goal of learning or viewing the teacher as the keeper of "the truth." We need to move to new attitudes about knowledge where the content or information offered by the teacher, textbook, or other expert is never taken at face value,

> Questions are the fuel we need to help us develop as thinkers.

but is always viewed as a starting point for wondering. After all, curiosity is what motivates learning (see *Figure 9: Questions that drive learning*).

Questions also fuel the daily social interactions in our classrooms. It is a pretty dull class where no one is asking interesting questions or where the only requirement is to answer superficial and surface content questions. Most teachers want to develop classroom spaces where students want to know what other students know—their opinions, beliefs, and desires. Students should be encouraged to question together and to experience first-hand the diversity of thinking, beliefs, and experiences in the classroom.

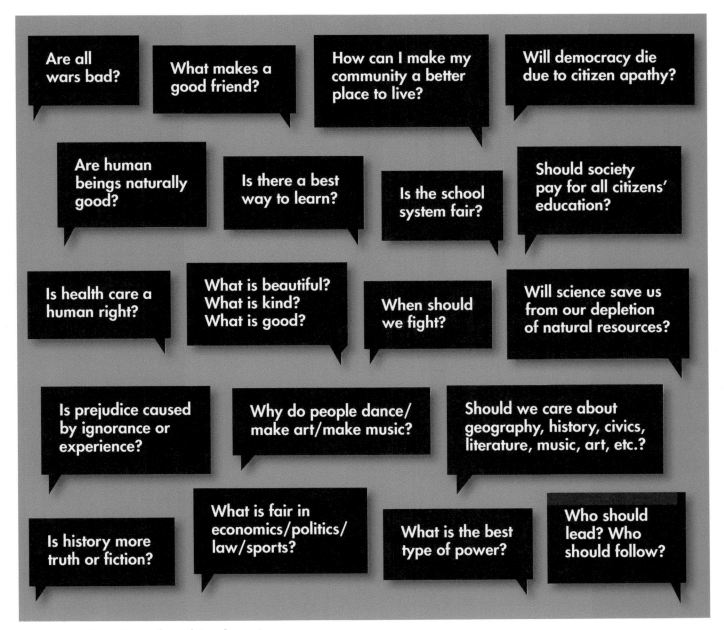

FIGURE 9: **Questions that drive learning**

In our day-to-day planning, we try to think of ways to encourage our students to become critical thinkers, skilled at asking insightful questions that challenge lazy thinking and *status quo* beliefs. At the same time, we try to nurture creative thinkers who are skilled at asking questions that open the mind and push towards new possibilities. This may seem like a tall order at times, especially given the high number of content expectations.

Learning how to learn

So why should you make questioning a focus of your course? Why is it important for students to become better questioners? Students today are consumers of information and can easily leverage technology to meet their need for information. The school is no longer required as a place that "gives" information to students. Schools today are finding a new focus on being a place to learn *how to learn* instead of a place to get *what to learn*.

As schools grapple with this new purpose of learning how to learn, students continue to be sophisticated consumers and producers of information in a digital age. They need to question information for a number of reasons: to assess the source of the information; to analyze the information; to seek opposing information; and to monitor their thinking as a consumer of information, with questions such as "Why do I believe this person/source?" or "What assumptions does this person/source make?"

Equally important, students also need to question how and why they produce information to be shared with members of diverse digital communities: "How did I arrive at my conclusion for my blog comment?" "Why do I feel it is important for me to share these ideas with other people?" "How can I involve other people in further investigation of this topic?" As consumers and producers of information, students need practice at asking thoughtful, relevant, analytical, and ethical questions.

It may be just as important for teachers to become better questioners. Our skill at questioning fuels how we think about our students, our subject areas, and our beliefs about teaching and learning. It is easy to spot a teacher who is passionate about their subject. They have an enthusiastic ability to ask questions and urge others to do the same.

Before considering the elements of a good inquiry question, examine the *Quotes to Consider: Questions are the core of learning* feature to further your thinking on the relationship of questioning to learning.

> Schools today are finding a new focus on being a place to learn *how to learn* instead of a place to get *what to learn*.

Questions are the core of learning

"We must continually remind ourselves that thinking begins with respect to some content only when questions are generated by both teachers and students. No questions equals no understanding. Superficial questions equal superficial understanding. Most students typically have no questions. They not only sit in silence, their minds are silent as well. Hence, the questions they do have tend to be superficial and ill-informed. This demonstrates that most of the time they are not thinking through the content they are presumed to be learning. This demonstrates that most of the time they are not learning the content they are presumed to be learning."

"Feeding students endless content to remember (that is, declarative sentences to remember) is akin to repeatedly stepping on the brakes in a vehicle that is, unfortunately, already at rest. Instead, students need questions to turn on their intellectual engines and they need to generate questions from our questions to get their thinking to go somewhere. Thinking is of no use unless it goes somewhere, and again, the questions we ask determine where our thinking goes."

—Richard Paul and Linda Elder, *Critical Thinking* (2000)

"In a world of coverage, the purpose of a question is to seek information and check recall. We would expect—and we typically find—that most questions are low-level convergent knowledge and comprehension questions, whether asked by students, teachers, or textbooks: What is...? What are the steps of...? Who was...? When did...occur? What is the homework? How do you...? What do we need to know for the quiz? How long does it have to be? More open questions and lengthy discussions, rather than being welcomed, can thus be seen as tangents or hindrances to coverage!"

—Jay McTighe and Grant Wiggins, *Essential Questions* (2013)

Q What ideas presented in the quotes do you find challenging and why?

Q Do you agree with the assumptions and arguments of Paul, Elder, McTighe, and Wiggins?

Q Think about how curiosity is nurtured or discouraged in our classrooms, our communities, and our lives. Is your own curiosity as a teacher nurtured or discouraged?

Q What further questions do you have regarding your role as a teacher who wants students to be able to ask and pursue deep questions?

3.2 What does a good inquiry question look like?

The first step in initiating inquiry-based learning in your classroom is to formulate good discipline-based inquiry questions for your course or course unit. Why is this an important starting place for better pedagogical practice? In their book *Essential Questions*, Jay McTighe and Grant Wiggins (2013) give several good reasons:

- The use of questions signals to students that inquiry is the goal of learning in your class, and makes it more likely that a unit of study will be intellectually engaging.

- The use of questions forces us to clarify and prioritize what is truly important in terms of learning outcomes for our students.

For the purposes of this book, we will focus on developing questioning that relates specifically to an inquiry. A selection of inquiry questions for history, social studies, geography, and civics has been provided to help you think about the kinds of questions that may entice your students to think deeply about the core concepts and supporting content of your discipline. As you read the questions, identify the core concepts and consider the supporting content that you would use to pursue this inquiry.

EXAMPLES

History and social studies inquiry questions

- Is history truth or fiction?
- How can we better understand the people of the past?
- How do we know what we know about the past?
- What are the significant characteristics of Canada's historical identity?

Developing effective inquiry questions

Previously, in Chapter 1, we outlined some of the fundamental qualities of a good question. These qualities are detailed in John Barell's book *Developing More Curious Minds* (2003):

- A good question is an invitation to think (not recall, summarize, or detail).

- A good question comes from genuine curiosity and confusion about the world.

- A good question makes you think about something in a way you never considered before.

- A good question invites both deep thinking and deep feelings.

- A good question leads to more good questions.

- A good question asks you to think critically, creatively, ethically, productively, and reflectively about essential ideas in a discipline.

McTighe and Wiggins (2013) propose similar criteria to Barell's, and add the following criteria. In their view, a good question:

- is open-ended; typically there is no final, correct answer

- points towards important, transferable ideas within (and sometimes across) disciplines

- requires support and justification; not just an answer
- recurs over time; the question should be revisited

Let's illustrate with an example. Perhaps you're thinking about changing your geography unit on the topic of land use in Canada from a content-oriented approach to an inquiry-based approach. You begin with the question, "What are the characteristics of land use in Canadian communities?" and then realize that this question asks only for content recall and can be answered through an Internet or textbook search.

You then revise the question to "What is the significance of land use in Canada?" and then think the question is too similar to the first and that student responses to the question may not involve the expected level of critical thought.

You take another shot and come up with, "What are the key characteristics that help create a livable community?" You wonder if students will be engaged by that question. You sense that the question has potential since you can envision some of the great source material and community guest speakers that would make the inquiry come to life for students and allow for deep thinking and feeling.

Finally, after much thought and a discussion with a colleague, you settle on the question:

How can we create more livable communities?

You feel that this question will engage students' genuine curiosity. The question is an invitation to think and take action, not to simply recall, summarize, or detail facts. The question also leads to more good questions. You think about the types of cases that the students may want to investigate in order to answer the question, such as current community land-use issues.

> An inquiry question is an invitation to think and take action, not to simply recall, summarize, or detail facts.

Integrating inquiry questions into your course

We suggest that you create four to five inquiry questions to ground a course, although there is no formula for the number of inquiry questions in a course. For every unit of study of significant length (over two weeks of time), you may require two to three additional questions that reflect both a specific topic/theme or core concepts of the course. The inquiry questions that ground your course should be reflected in most of the unit inquiry questions, but not necessarily all of them.

When you draft your course and unit inquiry questions, check to see that they align. If they do not, you may want to revise or drop some of your questions. Some teachers want to know if students should be the creators of the unit questions. As the teacher, you have the required expertise in the discipline and know how to pose an intellectually engaging question that will keep the learning moving forward. As students get more skilled at inquiry-based learning, they can certainly be expected to create additional questions to guide their inquiry (see Section 3.3, p. 50).

You do not have to pose inquiry questions for every lesson or each activity. If there are too many layers of inquiry questions, students may lose focus and become confused as to which question is the most important for them to answer.

So where can you go for help with creating inquiry questions? Curriculum documents, textbooks, and other resources often provide inquiry questions and/or big ideas and concepts that can be adapted into powerful inquiry questions.

We suggest working with colleagues to create overarching course inquiry questions that connect closely to core concepts. By working through the fundamental question "Why is _____ (history, geography, and so on) important?" along with mandated curriculum documents, you and your colleagues who teach the same subject can create powerful course questions. The process involves working through what you believe to be important essential skills, core concepts, and supportive content. This challenging stage can take some time and effort, but may result in greater student engagement and achievement.

A case study on p. 47 highlights the beginning of a collegial conversation about inquiry questions for a history course. *Figure 10: Inquiry-focused course overview—Civics* provides suggested course inquiry questions, unit inquiry questions, core concepts, and critical content for a course in civics. What strengths do you see in the proposed civics inquiry model? What challenges? What changes would you propose?

ENSURING SUCCESS

Making questions visible

Course inquiry questions should be posted in the classroom and included in written course outlines so that students can immediately see that they will have to think through the answers—not memorize provided answers. Course inquiry questions can also be used as sections in student portfolios and as final assessment questions in end-of-course or unit evaluations.

Course inquiry question	Unit of study inquiry questions	Core concepts	Critical content
If you didn't live in Canada, would you want to?	Are you a good citizen? Is citizenship about more than where you were born? Is Canada a great country to live in?	citizenship, identity	■ Canadian citizenship and identity ■ active citizenship ■ fundamental beliefs and values of democracy ■ changing views of citizenship ■ global citizenship
How should we balance individual rights and the common good?	Should governments limit individual rights and freedoms for the common good? What can and should happen when rights are abused?	common good, human rights	■ rights of Canadians ■ how rights relate to the common good ■ conflicts between rights and the common good ■ standing up for rights ■ rights abuses
How should our government work?	Should our government be more democratic? Should our government do more or less?	government, power	■ how government works ■ left- and right-wing perspectives ■ how different beliefs and values affect government ■ Canadian political spectrum ■ how government affects our lives ■ Aboriginal self-government ■ electoral system ■ deciding who to vote for ■ voter apathy ■ ways to influence government
Is our justice system just?	Can one justice system look after everyone's interests? What can and should be done when the system fails?	justice, equality	■ Canadian justice system ■ criminal and civil law ■ problems and challenges within the justice system
Want change? What should you do about it?	Would you act to right a wrong? Is illegal action ever justified to bring about a desired change?	power, privilege, activism	■ active citizenship ■ attributes and examples of an active citizen ■ legal means to bring about change ■ illegal actions to bring about change

FIGURE 10: Inquiry-focused course overview—Civics

SOURCE: Course inquiry and investigation questions adapted from *Canadian Investigations: Civics and Citizenship*, Oxford University Press (2014).

Creating powerful inquiry questions

Sean, Matt, and Elisha are teaching Canadian history at the secondary level this year. They are working together to create inquiry questions for the course. They have already decided on two overriding course questions that focus on historical evidence, historical significance, and Canadian identity:

1. How do we know what we know about Canada's past?
2. What are the significant characteristics of Canada's historical identity?

ELISHA: *I've always taught the course chronologically, like the curriculum suggests, so I have five units to plan for.*

SEAN: *I tried a thematic approach last year and I had five units as well. I think thematic works better for an inquiry focus. I know you feel differently.*

MATT: *Well, I did the same as Elisha and I find the kids get confused with themes since they are bouncing all over the decades. Elisha and I have themes within our chronology. Why don't we record our unit titles on some chart paper and see if we can work up some decent questions to start?*

	Matt and Elisha's chronological units	Sean's thematic units
Unit 1	WWI, 1920s and 30s	Canada and the world
Unit 2	WWII	French–English relations
Unit 3	1946–1968	Aboriginal perspectives
Unit 4	1968–1984	Technological, economic, and social change
Unit 5	1984–present	Canada today

FIGURE 11: Chronological and thematic units

ELISHA: *Wow, this looks completely different. Maybe we can start with a possible inquiry question for Unit 5 since they seem the most similar.*

SEAN: *Okay, so what are the central ideas that will get kids thinking about Canada today but link to our past?*

MATT: *Probably identity. You know...is there a Canadian identity? Maybe something about immigration, technology, and the economy?*

continued

ELISHA: *Maybe the question should ask them to consider Canada's future in some way?*

SEAN: *How about, "What will my life be like in Canada ten years from now?" or "How will Canada change and how will it be the same in 20 years?"*

ELISHA: *I like the first one! It makes it personal and not too far in the future to become unmanageable.*

MATT: *So would we provide them with current sources on immigration, economy, and technology issues and let them choose what to investigate?*

SEAN: *That could work. The question does help to consolidate the learning in the course and it ties in to our second overall course question. It focuses on change and continuity as well, which are important concepts. Maybe the second question is better, I'm not sure.*

MATT: *Well, let's leave that one for now. For our unit on the Depression and WWII last year, we asked the questions "Who and what was to blame for WWII?" and "How did Canada change as a result of the war?" I think we can stick to those. What do you do for your "Canada and the world" unit, Sean?*

SEAN: *I focus on peace, conflict, and prosperity. I didn't use any inquiry questions, just topics for research on the war, the Cold War era, and peacekeeping era. Thinking about it now, something like "When should Canada fight?" or "When should Canada have fought?" would be interesting. Kids could look at WWII, the Korean War, peacekeeping, the war in Afghanistan, our refusal to join the US in Iraq, as well as the genocide in Rwanda or the conflict in Syria. That would work for me.*

ELISHA: *I really like that idea. Maybe we should try one of Sean's questions, Matt. What do you think?*

MATT: *I'm not sure I want to give up all the stuff we created last year, plus the textbook is chronological. The kids really did well on our unit last year. Do we have to do the same thing?*

SEAN: *Maybe not, but it would be good to compare our students' work and be able to discuss their progress in the inquiries.*

	Chronological units	Possible inquiry questions	Thematic units	Possible inquiry questions
Unit 1	WWI, 1920s and 30s	Were the sacrifices of Canadians in WWI justified? Who prospers when and why?	Canada and the world	Was and is Canada a peaceful nation? Should Canada have fought?
Unit 2	WWII	Did Canada emerge as a stronger or weaker country after WWII? Who or what was to blame for causing WWII?	French–English relations	Should Quebec separate? Is English Canada unfairly privileged?
Unit 3	1946–1968	Was Canada a peaceful nation? How did technology change us? Should the Canadian government have taken on more responsibilities for its citizens?	Aboriginal perspectives	Can Aboriginal peoples reclaim what they have lost? Should the present-day government address historic wrongs? How can Aboriginal peoples and non-Aboriginal peoples co-exist as equals?
Unit 4	1968–1984	Which event during this period made the most significant contribution to Canadian identity? What impact has regionalism had on Canada?	Technological, economic, and social change	Why do times of change cause both conflict and cooperation? What factors contributed to the development of social movements in Canada?
Unit 5	1984–present	What impact has changing demographics had on different groups in Canada? Where do you see yourself in the Canadian narrative?	Canada today	Is Canada a first-rate or second-rate country? Should Canada be a good global citizen? What will my life be like as a Canadian, ten years from now?

FIGURE 12: **The result—Working draft of inquiry questions in Canadian history**

Q What are the assumptions and arguments of Matt, Elisha, and Sean? Do you share or challenge these assumptions and/or arguments?

Q Consider the suggested course structure, unit structure, and inquiry questions and critique them. Suggest revisions or alternatives.

Q Create and revise as many inquiry questions as appropriate for a course that you teach.

3.3

How can I help my students develop their own inquiry questions?

Think back to Richard Paul and Linda Elder's (2000) observation about students' silent minds on p. 41 and your own classroom experience. If students have lost their natural curiosity and ability to ask questions, inquiry-based learning may help to revive these dispositions. At first you may be frustrated by students' attempts to get you to provide both the questions and the answers, but with time and practice, students should regain a questioning disposition.

One good place to start is to present students with a brief list and have them identify with a simple "yes" or "no" which questions they think are good inquiry questions. Ensure students have the criteria for a good inquiry question as they make their selections.

> If students have lost their natural curiosity and ability to ask questions, inquiry-based learning may help to revive these dispositions.

EXAMPLES

Questions to teach questioning

1. What are examples of teenage rebellion?
2. Should teenagers rebel?
3. What television shows feature rebellious teenagers?
4. How many people in prison are teenagers?
5. How is the teenage brain different?
6. Do we need specific laws for teenagers?

In a debrief, you would point out that questions one, three, four, and five are factual questions with correct answers (although it could be argued that number five is a scientific question that has yet to be answered!). Question two is a good inquiry question, despite its simplicity, since it is thought-provoking, open ended, and sparks further questions. Question six is not a yes-or-no opinion question; it is a question that demands support and justification and is also a good inquiry question.

After this preliminary activity, the next step may be to have students brainstorm two to three further questions that focus on the lives of teenagers to see if they can apply what they have learned. At this stage, it is important to listen to the students' justification for their questions. While a question may seem to miss the mark, understanding students' intent can reveal how to turn a question from a simple factual or opinion-based question into a solid inquiry question.

> **EXAMPLE**
>
> *Do teenagers commit more crimes than adults?*
>
> … can be changed to:
>
> *Should teenagers be held just as accountable for their crimes as adults?*

You may also want to caution students against creating leading questions (these are also very hard to avoid as a teacher). A leading question suggests the answer. See *Figure 13* for examples of leading questions that you could discuss with students. Ask them to suggest more neutral (less biased) versions of these questions.

Leading question	Neutral question
Why was Germany to blame for WWII?	Where does the responsibility lie for the events of WWII?
Should violent teens face harsher punishments than adults?	Is justice the same for teens and adults?
Why would Parliament benefit from more women MPs?	Should gender equity be a consideration of parliamentary representation?
Why is Canada a more peaceful nation than the US?	When should a country fight?

FIGURE 13: **Leading and neutral questions**

Students should practise creating and revising possible inquiry questions arising from provocative sources such as websites, photographs, quotations, media, and print texts throughout all stages of the inquiry process, not just in the beginning. (For example, students can use *Reproducible 4: Asking Questions about Photographs* on p. 140 when gathering visual information from the web or other media.)

REPRODUCIBLE 4: Asking Questions about Photographs

Name: ______________________________ Date: __________________

Inquiry focus: ____

Work collaboratively through the following steps to try to create deep questions based on your thinking about the photograph.

1. Have a discussion about what you observe is happening and what you infer is happening.
2. Each person in the group should create 3 to 5 questions based on your curiosities arising from the photograph.
3. After everyone has a list of preliminary questions, collaborate to choose 3 of these initial questions to "perfect" them into deep inquiry questions.
4. For each of your "perfected" questions, list 2 or 3 additional questions that arise from the perfected questions.

1. This is what we see in the photograph (observations):

   ____

   This is what we infer from what we see in the photograph (inferences):

   ____

2. My questions about the photograph:

   ____

3.

Our top 3 deep inquiry questions	Do our 3 questions meet these criteria for a deep inquiry question?
1.	❑ An invitation to think (not recall, summarize, or detail). You can't find the answer through a simple Internet search. ❑ Requires support and justification, not just an answer. ❑ Open-ended; typically there is no final, correct answer. ❑ Arises from genuine curiosity and confusion about the world. ❑ Makes you think about something in a way you never considered before. ❑ Invites both deep thinking and deep feelings. Asks you to think ethically (what is right and wrong). ❑ Leads to more good questions.
2.	
3.	

4. Additional questions that arise from the deep inquiry questions:

   ____

140 Reproducibles *IQ: A Practical Guide to Inquiry-based Learning*

FIGURE 14: Reproducible 4

The following ideas are offered as additional ways to encourage student awareness of questioning as essential to learning:

- ☑ Post course questions in a conspicuous place.
- ☑ Post and feature students' questions. Feature a "question of the day." Create a classroom culture where all learners feel valued and respected in order to optimize curiosity (provide opportunities for students to get to know each other and ask questions of each other's thinking).
- ☑ Model ways to ask questions about the media, ideas, behaviours, and your discipline.
- ☑ Provide students with *Reproducible 5: Asking Questions about Sources* on p. 141 where they can record questions that arise after a

discussion, after viewing a source, or after hearing a community speaker.

- ☑ Have students write and revise their own inquiry questions in their inquiry journal (see p. 75).

- ☑ Post quotes from diverse thinkers expressing their thinking about the nature of questioning. (See p. 142 for *Reproducible 6: Quotes about Questions*. Have students consider the quotes and answer the questions provided in the reproducible.)

REPRODUCIBLE 5: Asking Questions about Sources

Name: _____ Date: _____

Speaker/Source: _____

Answer the following questions individually.

1. What is your purpose in asking questions of this person or sourc
   _____
   _____

2. What are your questions?
   _____
   _____

3. What types of questions have you asked?
   _____
   _____
   _____

Answer the following questions in a group.

4. Compare your questions with those of other students. What pa
   do the questions reveal?
   _____
   _____

5. How do the questions link to important concepts and content
   _____
   _____

6. How could you improve one of your questions?
   _____
   _____
   _____

IQ: A Practical Guide to Inquiry-based Learning

FIGURE 15: Reproducible 5

REPRODUCIBLE 6: Quotes about Questions

Name: _____ Date: _____

Individually reflect on the following quotes and answer these questions.

1. Consider what ideas in the quotes you agree with and provide examples of the quotes' relevance to your life inside and outside the classroom. Use the questions at the bottom of the page to stimulate your thinking.
2. Think about why questioning will be important in this classroom and how we can improve as questioners.
3. Join with a partner to discuss your thoughts. Note how your conversation with a partner was different after thinking about questioning.

"The most important question in the world is, 'Why is the child crying?'" **Alice Walker**

"The power to question is the basis of all human progress." **Indira Gandhi**

"It is better to debate a question without settling it than to settle a question without debating it." **Joseph Joubert**

"Life's most persistent and urgent question is, 'What are you doing for others?'" **Martin Luther King Jr.**

"The question isn't who is going to let me; it's who is going to stop me." **Ayn Rand**

"If love is the answer, could you please rephrase the question?" **Lily Tomlin**

"A wise man can learn more from a foolish question than a fool can learn from a wise answer." **Bruce Lee**

"The great question that has never been answered, and which I have not yet been able to answer, despite my thirty years of research into the feminine soul, is 'What does a woman want?'" **Sigmund Freud**

1. What concept is at the root of these quotes?
2. Some of the quotes are asking questions. What "type" of question is being asked? Ethical? Political? Social? Philosophical?
3. What does the person being quoted believe is the importance of questions?
4. Which quotes resonate with you and why?
5. Which quotes trouble you and why?

142 Reproducibles   *IQ: A Practical Guide to Inquiry-based Learning*

FIGURE 16: Reproducible 6

3.4

How can I use questions to help my students analyze their thinking?

Inquiry-based learning requires considerable amounts of analytical thinking, which may pose challenges for many students. We can't just ask students to "think harder"—we need to describe explicitly what good thinking involves, and encourage students to think about their own thinking even when we are not there.

On pp. 55–57, some key questions are provided that ask students to analyze the evidence and their own thinking. These analytical questions break down thinking (one's own thinking or thinking articulated in sources) into discrete parts that can be carefully examined. The questions have also been collected in *Reproducible 7: Questions to Assist Inquiry Thinking* on p. 143, which you can distribute to students.

So what are the discrete parts of thinking? In their work on critical thinking, Paul and Elder (2010) identify eight universal elements that can be used to analyze and improve thinking (see *Figure 17: Eight universal elements of thought*). The eight elements of thought help students keep their own thinking processes at the forefront of their inquiry.

Developing an inquiry with your students

The following is an example of how a teacher could pose key questions that capture the eight elements of thought.

Let's say you pose an overarching inquiry question: "How can Aboriginal peoples and non-Aboriginal peoples co-exist as equals in Canada?" You explain to the students that they will be examining the ways in which Aboriginal peoples and non-Aboriginal peoples in Canada have co-existed, cooperated, and experienced significant conflict. You note that there are different perspectives on what co-existence could look like—socially, politically, and economically—and whether or not co-existence is the goal of different Aboriginal groups and non-Aboriginal groups.

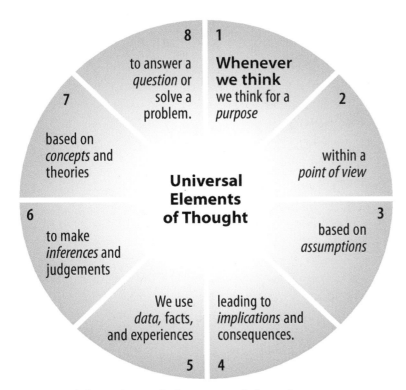

FIGURE 17: Eight universal elements of thought

SOURCE: Paul, Richard, and Elder, Linda, *The Miniature Guide to the Art of Asking Essential Questions*, Foundation for Critical Thinking (2010).

You introduce the final culminating activity, a persuasive essay and visual display of conclusions, and explain that community members, including those from local Native Friendship centres, will be in attendance for final presentations of student conclusions.

You check in to see if students understand the purpose of the inquiry by discussing the following questions:

Questions that unpack the inquiry

- Why do we care about this issue?

- What do we hope to find out?

- How will we proceed to answer the question/solve the problem?

The next stage of thinking involves a careful consideration of the inquiry question and questions arising from it. You may provide more content-specific questions, or the students, depending on their experience and proficiency, may develop their own questions (e.g., "Is there agreement among Aboriginal peoples about what equality looks like?" "What does the Canadian government think equality for Aboriginal peoples looks like?" "Have Aboriginal peoples been treated fairly and equally?" "Does the residential school experience prove that Aboriginal and non-Aboriginal peoples cannot co-exist equally?"). You would carefully track and assess the creation of such additional questions.

Next, you point out to students that the most basic concept in the overarching question is equality. You plan activities where students get to think about what equality means in social, political, and economic terms. Students should be able to answer the question "What is equality?" as it relates specifically to the inquiry question. Every inquiry question should be predicated on a concept or concepts key to the discipline that can be unpacked through analytical questioning.

Questions that unpack concepts

- What is the main idea you are using in your thinking?
- Can you explain the concept to me?
- Is there a different concept that would work in considering this problem?

Students then consider what evidence they require to answer the question. Here are four analytical questions that teachers and students could use to question evidence and their own inferences as they consider evidence:

Questions that unpack evidence

- What is the source of this information?
- What is the quality of this information?
- Do I have all the information I need?
- How am I making meaning of this information?

You should check in with students on a regular basis during the inquiry process with questions that may help students reflect on their own assumptions or biases. These questions should ask students to articulate their inferences and conclusions and to think about the implications of their reasoning.

Questions that unpack reaching a conclusion

- What does the author or speaker take for granted?
- What am I taking for granted?
- What alternative assumptions are there to consider?

- What are the relevant points of view?
- What is my point of view?
- Can I explain my thinking?
- How did I reach my conclusion?
- Have I considered other alternative plausible conclusions?
- Where is this argument/conclusion/point of view leading us?
- What will happen if my conclusion is correct?

The guiding questions shown below in *Figure 18: Analytical questions based on the eight elements of thought* will also be helpful to you during the planning stage of an inquiry. Along with the questions in *Reproducible 7*, these questions can guide students and can also be used as important assessment information to help students improve their thinking. You could consider using some of these analytical questions in student portfolio work and conferencing.

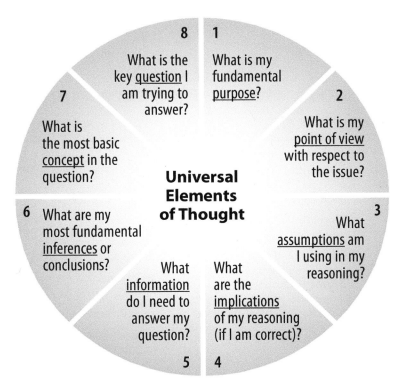

FIGURE 18: Analytical questions based on the eight elements of thought

Source: Paul, Richard, and Elder, Linda, *The Miniature Guide to the Art of Asking Essential Questions*, Foundation for Critical Thinking (2010).

3.5 How can I assess students as they create, refine, and ask further questions?

Chapter 2 provided some assessment strategies to help you gather evidence of student learning during an inquiry, including *Reproducible 3: Inquiry Assessment Planning Template* on p. 139. Below, *Figure 19: Assessment evidence from questioning* reproduces a section from that reproducible with additional suggestions for gathering reliable assessment evidence from questioning that arises from products, observations, and conversations. *Reproducible 8: Questioning Skills Rubric* is provided on p. 144 to help you assess students' overall achievement with questioning in their products, observations, and conversations.

Learning Goal	Ways to gather evidence of student learning		
	Products	**Observations**	**Conversations**
Questioning Student asks and refines relevant questions that further the investigation.	Student identifies good inquiry questions from a list of options and provides a written explanation of choice. Student creates a flow chart detailing changes to initial questions to the final revised question. Student answers analytical questions in their inquiry journal regarding a question such as: ■ From what viewpoint is this question? ■ From a different viewpoint, what could this question be? ■ From which perspective should we ask the question?	Observe student ranking various questions you have provided from deepest to superficial. Observe student peer assess questions. Observe student creating questions based on provocative quotes, photographs, statistical data, etc., that you have provided.	*What are you wondering about? What surprised you?* *What makes a good inquiry question?* *How does this question link to important concepts we have discussed?* *How could you improve this question?* *Can you explain this question?* *Is there a different/better question that could be posed?* *Could we phrase the question a different way?* *What is the ethical dimension of this question?*

FIGURE 19: Assessment evidence from questioning

REPRODUCIBLE 8: Questioning Skills Rubric

Name: _____ Date: _____

Inquiry focus: _____

Success Criteria Category	Exceptional	Good	Getting there	Not yet	Further support required
QUESTIONING **Inquiry Question** The student asks relevant questions that further the investigation.	Student applies understanding of the qualities of an effective inquiry question by consistently asking (and refining) inquiry questions.	Student applies understanding of the qualities of an effective inquiry question by frequently asking (and refining) inquiry questions.	Student applies understanding of the qualities of an effective inquiry question by asking (and refining) some inquiry questions.	Student is beginning to identify the qualities of an effective inquiry question but cannot yet apply their understanding to refining or asking their own inquiry questions.	Student needs further support in asking inquiry questions.
Questioning Thinking The student answers analysis questions accurately (i.e., identifying concepts, purpose, point of view, inferences, and assumptions) and refines their thinking based on their analysis.	Student consistently answers analysis questions accurately, refines their thinking, and sets reasonable learning goals based on their analysis.	Student frequently answers analysis questions accurately, refines their thinking, and sets reasonable learning goals based on their analysis.	Student sometimes answers analysis questions accurately, refines their thinking, and sets reasonable learning goals based on their analysis.	Student is beginning to accurately answer analysis questions, refine their thinking, and set learning goals based on their analysis.	Student needs further support in answering analysis questions accurately and setting reasonable learning goals.

Descriptive feedback and next steps:

My goals related to this feedback:

FIGURE 20: **Reproducible 8**

REVISIT AND REFLECT

This chapter looked closely at the purpose of questions in learning generally, and in inquiry-based learning specifically. Formulating good inquiry questions takes considerable thought and discipline expertise. Once you've created a good inquiry question, it can capture and hold student interest and propel their curiosity, thinking, and learning. Analytical questions, based on the elements of thinking, can help students distinguish "weak" thinking from "strong" thinking in both themselves and others. Ultimately, a classroom culture that encourages curiosity, risk-taking, open-mindedness, and persistence fosters a questioning mindset. That mindset allows students to become proficient questioners beyond the classroom walls.

To conclude your exploration of this chapter, take some time to think through these questions:

Q What is one specific task that you can create to encourage students to question digital information analytically?

Q How do you promote curiosity in your subject matter specifically and in your classroom in general?

Q At this point in your planning, what powerful inquiry questions are you considering? What do these questions reveal about your values, beliefs, and assumptions about student interest and your subject area?

Q What do you think would be a fair and reliable way to assess students' questioning skills throughout an inquiry?

CHAPTER 4
IMPROVE
COMMUNICATION

4.1 What is the essential vocabulary of communicating inquiry thinking?

4.2 How do I purposefully attend to communication during an inquiry?

4.3 How can communication be assessed in a final product?

4.1

What is the essential vocabulary of communicating inquiry thinking?

Students engaged in an inquiry are working towards becoming better communicators. Whether asking questions, working collaboratively to evaluate the validity of a source, or confidently presenting new ideas at the end of the inquiry process, your students' skill at expressing and explaining their thinking is key to their success as learners.

This chapter will give you the opportunity to think through the types of communication skills that are at the core of inquiry-based learning and how to help students improve these skills. It addresses some essential vocabulary of communication, the purposes of student talk (both formal and informal), ways to improve communication, and using inquiry journals and teacher conferencing to improve skills and assess student thinking.

It is hard to not state the obvious: communication is the only way that students can make their learning visible to you and to other students. For this reason, it is essential to plan for multiple opportunities that allow students to communicate their thinking throughout the inquiry and in the products of inquiry.

> Your students' skill at expressing and explaining their thinking is key to their success as learners.

Categories of inquiry vocabulary

Explicit teaching of inquiry-based learning vocabulary includes inquiry "action words," or processes, concepts, and words to describe thinking, beliefs, ideas, and dispositions. The deliberate use of inquiry vocabulary helps to ensure that your students understand important inquiry strategies.

If a student does not understand the word "synthesize" or "logical," for example, she is at a disadvantage for a number of reasons. She cannot articulate the attributes of thinking that will lead to success as an inquiry learner. Also, feedback from the teacher or a peer (e.g., "Your argument is illogical") will be meaningless, and her ability to set goals for improvement will be compromised.

Students and teachers need exact words to describe the processes, types, and attributes of thinking in the sources that they are considering. A website may be described as "not very good," but that is far less meaningful than describing it as "unreliable" and "biased."

Students also need to be able to speak and write fluently about the concepts that are important to inquiry-based learning. Asking a student what his assumption is in an argument is only meaningful when he knows what "assumption" means, and why assumptions are important to his ability to make an effective argument.

Creating a culture of inquiry in your classroom requires you and your students to use essential inquiry vocabulary to build an understanding of inquiry and to describe each member of the classroom as an inquiry learner. The use and misuse of inquiry vocabulary gives you immediate evidence to determine if the student has preconceptions or misconceptions that must be addressed.

For example, a student may believe that the terms *synthesize* and *summarize* are the same. For this reason, the student may not be using the higher-level thinking skill required of synthesizing sources. He may simply be taking point-form notes of all sources with no attempt to combine the sources into more complex thought. A teacher that notes a student's misunderstanding of the word *synthesize* can provide immediate feedback and direction to put the learner back on track.

In your planning, consider using *Reproducible 9: Essential Inquiry Vocabulary* on p. 145 to introduce the terms that you and your students should be using in informal and formal conversations and in written work.

The suggested vocabulary is divided into four categories:

- Inquiry action words
- Concepts important to inquiry-based learning
- Words to describe thoughts, beliefs, and ideas
- Words to describe inquiry dispositions

The fourth category of inquiry—disposition vocabulary—is extremely significant since students may correctly understand terms in the context of goals and strategies for learning, but lack the necessary dispositions to achieve the learning. Students must be able to recognize in themselves and others the dispositions necessary to be an effective inquiry learner. To cultivate a curious classroom, teachers and students should be using words such as *perseverance*, *self-confidence*, and *open-mindedness* to describe those personal attitudes that will advance them as learners.

Students must be able to recognize in themselves and others the dispositions necessary to be an effective inquiry learner.

Name: _____ Date: _____

Inquiry action words	
question	To request information
clarify	To make something easier to understand
extend	To expand a meaning
defend	To speak or write in favour of a person, idea, or action
refute	To prove that something is wrong
assess	To evaluate the quality of (synonym: to evaluate)
analyze	To examine in detail to expand meaning
synthesize	To combine ideas to form a theory (overall explanation)
evaluate	To judge based on criteria (synonym: to assess, but often construed as a more demanding and exacting form of assessing)
persuade	To convince someone of your way of thinking
conclude	To infer on the basis of evidence

Words to describe thoughts, beliefs, and ideas	
logical	Clear, sound reasoning
coherent	Logical and consistent
effective	Capable of producing desired result
clear	Easy to understand, not confusing
precise	Exact, accurate, careful
reliable	Trustworthy
abstract	Something that is not a material object, typically an idea
concept	An idea that is connected to something abstract
practical	Connected to real situations rather than ideas or theories Likely to succeed if implemented
theoretical	Ideas on which a subject is based (rather than practical)
ethical	Beliefs about what is right and wrong
operable	Something that can be used
accurate	Correct and true
relevant	Closely connected to the subject under consideration
significant	Important enough to have an effect or to be noticed

Concepts important to inquiry-based learning	
inquiry	Asking questions and collecting information/evidence to answer the question
metacognition	Knowing about knowing (or thinking about thinking)
bias	To show prejudice
point of view	A particular attitude or way of considering
perspective	A mental view or outlook
implication	A possible effect or result of an action
assumption	A belief that something is true although there is no proof

Words to describe inquiry dispositions (from Reproducible 1: How to Model and Assess Inquiry Dispositions)	
curiosity	Teacher and students want to know more about the world and its people. They ask important, relevant, and deep questions. These questions are not answered easily, nor does the student or teacher have the correct answer in mind when they begin. They are honestly perplexed by the issue/question/problem and have the motivation to uncover a possible answer/solution.
self-confidence	Teacher and students trust that they can figure out difficult problems by using their reason and intelligence.
flexible thinker	Teacher and students are willing to try out different types of thinking (i.e., political thinking, creative thinking, critical thinking, and reflective thinking) and different points of view.
open-mindedness	Teacher and students are genuinely interested in other perspectives and attitudes. They realize that the question is never fully answered and that knowledge is always being constructed. They are open to continual learning.
perseverance	Teacher and students are not put off by obstacles and challenges in their learning.
taking risks	Teacher and students are not looking for one correct answer but are more playful and creative in thinking. They are confident that their thinking is a "work in progress" and are open to new ways of thinking and learning that may be outside their area of expertise/comfort/skill.
reflection	Teacher and students think about their thinking and know why it is important to do so. They can self- and peer assess products. They can make connections to their personal lives and identity as well as to the broader world.

FIGURE 21: **Reproducible 9**

ENSURING SUCCESS

English language learners

English language learners especially benefit when inquiry vocabulary is directly taught and modelled by the teacher and other students, and when there is immediate and regular assessment for learning feedback.

Strategies for implementing inquiry vocabulary

Here are some practical ideas on weaving inquiry vocabulary into your daily classroom tasks. Over time, you should notice a new and powerful common language being spoken by your students that will accelerate their ability to move towards independent inquiry.

1. Create "anchor charts" or "word walls" of key inquiry vocabulary. Students can provide sentences in their own words that demonstrate the meanings of the words. Post them in conspicuous places in the classroom. Refer to them and revise them often.

EXAMPLES

The following is a sample anchor chart with possible student responses to the question, "What is an inquiry?"

- Trying to find out the truth.
- Defending our solution to a critical problem.
- Checking out how other people have answered a question, and then answering it for myself.
- Searching for different ways of looking at an issue before I make up my mind.
- Thinking deeply about an important problem and making a conclusion.
- Questioning the world around us and wondering how it came to be this way and how it could be different.

2. As one component of an inquiry journal (see p. 75), have students articulate their understanding of two to three key inquiry vocabulary words in relation to their learning, not as discrete terminology.

EXAMPLES

Sample journal prompts

- As you prepare to look for the best sources for your research, how will you determine which are the most **reliable** and **relevant**?
- Create three potential inquiry questions on this topic. Which question has the most **clarity**? Which question is **unbiased**? Which question is most **precise**?
- Consider two opposing viewpoints that you have heard or read about the topic. Which viewpoint seems most **credible** to you and why? In what ways has the person attempted to **persuade** you of his or her viewpoint?
- How are you remaining **open-minded** as you gather and assess evidence?

3. When listening to collaborative groups at work, ask questions that invite students to explain their understanding of key inquiry vocabulary in relation to the work they are completing.

> **EXAMPLES**
>
> *"Have you considered everyone's* **point of view***?"*
>
> *"What* **assumption(s)** *were presented in this source? What* **assumptions** *are you making?"*
>
> *"What* **conclusions** *are you drawing from your discussions? What are the* **implications** *of the conclusions?"*

4. When conferencing with students regarding their inquiry work, probe their understanding of key inquiry vocabulary.
5. Have students collaboratively create metaphors for key inquiry vocabulary words. Have them apply their understanding of inquiry thinking and thinkers to life outside the classroom.

> **EXAMPLES**
>
> ■ What is an inquiry like?
>
> ■ What does perseverance look like in gaming? In basketball? In playing an instrument?
>
> ■ Who are some real-life inquiry thinkers? What makes them inquiry thinkers?
>
> ■ Who are some inquiry thinkers in popular television, movies, and on the Internet?

6. Students can create T-charts, Venn diagrams, or other key visuals to define key inquiry vocabulary words or to compare two or more key inquiry vocabulary words.

Point of view	Assumptions

Logical — Plausible — Justifiable

7. Create inquiry vocabulary "check-ins" by asking students comprehension and application questions. You can create the questions or alternatively, you can ask students to create questions on specific terms and have them assess each other.

EXAMPLES

1. Which of the following sentences **best** describes an **assumption**?

   a) What the writer/speaker takes for granted in their thinking.
   b) A strong argument proposed as a solution to a problem.
   c) A point of view.
   d) A wrong idea.

2. Which of the following statements is most **logical**?

   a) Parliament should pass a law to allow 15–17 year-olds to vote to make them active citizens.
   b) He's too old to be taken seriously.
   c) If we allow gay people to get married, then the institution of marriage will be destroyed.
   d) More environmental laws along with more environmental actions by citizens would help to preserve our environment for future generations.

3. When assessing sources of evidence to answer your question, which of the following is **most important** to **assess**?

   a) How persuasive the source is.
   b) How precise the source is.
   c) How current the source is.
   d) How credible the source is.

4.2 How do I purposefully attend to communication during an inquiry?

How can we best support communication skills through inquiry-based learning tasks? Let's begin by considering oral language in particular. A respectful classroom environment where diverse learners are valued is key, since students do not want to talk in a setting where their communication may be judged as wrong or inadequate.

Conversation

Many students come to high school with lots of experience in group work settings. Teachers must determine how skilled students are in purposeful and collaborative classroom talk and build on those skills accordingly. In the inquiry-based learning classroom, students make sense together. Conversations are the only way to allow this learning to happen. Be mindful that opportunities for student talk related to the inquiry must be planned, encouraged, and nurtured in each and every class.

Conversations also promote oral language skills. Conversations can vary in their degree of formality and use of protocols. Typically, students can benefit from a range of protocols to assist in their development of oral language and listening skills. Some of these common techniques include posing a question; allowing students time to think independently—then sharing their ideas with a partner to further develop them; and assigning specific roles in collaborative group discussions and using protocols that foster respect in whole-class discussions.

Here are some techniques that promote oral communication skills during whole-class discussions and, in some cases, collaborative group work:

☑ Arrange the classroom so that students can see each other's faces and encourage them to talk to each other, not just to you.

> In the inquiry-based learning classroom, students make sense together.

☑ Consider posing one or two key questions the day before the discussion, allowing students who require more "thinking" time to offer an answer.

☑ To encourage active engagement, set a time limit for whole-group discussions and let students know the limit.

☑ Develop a method where students' names are chosen at random to answer questions (use this technique only after the students know each other well).

☑ Allow students to "pass" if they cannot offer an answer, but always return to that student at some point of the discussion.

☑ Be sure to give enough wait time between asking a question and calling on a specific student to answer (minimum three to five seconds).

☑ For higher-order questions that have just been posed, give students time to individually process a response (encourage students to take jot notes for two to three minutes).

☑ As much as possible, do not repeat what students have said since this habit may make students focus on the teacher and not on their peers.

☑ Occasionally, ask students to complete a reflection. You can use *Reproducible 10: Today's Discussion Exit Card* on p. 146.

Listening

An inquiry classroom is a place where curious learners build knowledge together. The capacity to attend fully to other voices allows us to consider other ideas, react to them (extend, modify, adopt, or reject), and form our own beliefs and conclusions. Encourage students to think about their listening skills before engaging in sustained purposeful talk.

Active listening is a challenging skill to master, especially in conversations where we spend a lot of time mentally preparing our responses rather than attending to the person who is speaking. Listening can be particularly difficult when we are tired, when there are many distractions, when we are uninterested in the topic, and when we dislike or disagree with the person's position.

Laura Lipton and Bruce Wellman (2003), whose research includes learning-focused relationships, propose three distinct types of self-centered or egocentric listening that may interfere with our ability

REPRODUCIBLE 10: Today's Discussion Exit Card

Name: ______________________ Date: ______________

Topic being discussed: ______________________

1. How did you contribute to today's discussion? Add a comment beneath the choices that you check off.
   - ☐ I asked a question that related to a preceding idea.
   - ☐ I made a comment that showed interest in what someone else said.
   - ☐ I made a connection between two ideas.
   - ☐ I used body language to support other speakers.
   - ☐ I built on someone else's thoughts.
   - ☐ I disagreed in a respectful way.
2. What one important idea from today's discussion changed your thinking?
3. Think about the class as a whole. What can we do to improve the quality of our discussion?

146 Reproducibles *IQ: A Practical Guide to Inquiry-based Learning*

FIGURE 22: **Reproducible 10**

to fully attend to the voice of another in collaborative problem-solving and reflection conversations.

Personal referencing

This type of listening quickly moves from consideration of what is being said to judgmental responses based on your own beliefs. "I agree!" "I would never think about it like that." "I think that..."

Personal curiosity

This type of listening is motivated by our interest in wanting more information for ourselves instead of allowing the problem/issue/reflection to be fully understood. Personal curiosity is an important aspect of an inquiry classroom but it shouldn't disrupt a speaker who is trying to make her thinking understood. "What websites did you use?" "How did you figure that out?"

Personal certainty

This type of listening occurs when the listener quickly offers their own beliefs or solutions, often before the problem is fully understood and without fully considering all alternatives. "Have you thought about...?" "It's pretty obvious to me that...."

Share the descriptions and examples of these three types of "egocentric" listening with students and have them reflect on their own listening skills and those of other people. Another possible activity is included in *Reproducible 11: Quotes about Listening* on p. 147.

REPRODUCIBLE 11: Quotes about Listening

Name: _____   Date: _____

Individually reflect on the following quotes and answer these questions.

1. Consider what ideas you agree with, and provide examples of the quotes' relevance to your life inside and outside the classroom.
2. Think about why listening will be important in this classroom and how we can improve as listeners.
3. Join with a partner to discuss your thoughts. Note how your conversation with a partner was different after thinking about listening.

> "When I get ready to talk to people, I spend two thirds of the time thinking what they want to hear and one third thinking about what I want to say." **Abraham Lincoln**

> "People love to talk but hate to listen. Listening is not merely not talking, though even that is beyond most of our powers; it means taking a vigorous, human interest in what is being told us. You can listen like a blank wall or like a splendid auditorium where every sound comes back fuller and richer." **Alice Duer Miller**

> "This is the problem with dealing with someone who is actually a good listener. They don't jump in on your sentences, saving you from actually finishing them, or talk over you, allowing what you do manage to get out to be lost or altered in transit. Instead, they wait, so you have to keep going." **Sarah Dessen**

IQ: A Practical Guide to Inquiry-based Learning   Reproducibles **147**

FIGURE 23: Reproducible 11

Students could use *Reproducible 12: Listening Self-Assessment* on p. 148 following a collaborative group discussion about their own listening abilities, to consider areas of improvement. They can also be assigned as "fishbowl" observers and use *Reproducible 13: Fishbowl Observation* on p. 149 to provide feedback to their peers and to reflect on their own skill level.

REPRODUCIBLE 12: Listening Self-Assessment

Name: _____ Date: _____

Topic being discussed: _____

Complete this reflection following a lengthy discussion in a collaborative group.

I maintained eye contact with the person speaking.
Yes!   Most of the time   Not yet

My facial expressions and body language communicated interest, openness, and respect.
Yes!   Most of the time   Not yet

I was quiet when others were talking and I did not interrupt.
Yes!   Most of the time

I paraphrased other people's ideas and used their ideas to mak[e] connections to my own ideas.
Yes!   Most of the time

I avoided, as much as possible, "inner chatter" in my mind that i[nterfered] with attentive listening.
Yes!   Most of the time

Next steps:
_____
_____
_____
_____
_____
_____
_____
_____
_____

148 Reproducibles   IQ: A Pra[ctical]

FIGURE 24: Reproducible 12

REPRODUCIBLE 13: Fishbowl Observation

Name: _____ Date: _____

Topic being discussed: _____

You have been chosen to observe a group conversation carefully (like watching fish in a fishbowl).

For the following criteria, record one specific example that you observe. Be prepared to provide specific and respectful feedback to the group following your observation.

1. Participants build on each other's thinking.
   _____

2. Participants are respectful of each other.
   _____

3. Participants encourage alternative points of view and perspectives.
   _____

4. Participants engage in active listening (eye contact, body posture, giving verbal acknowledgements of each other's points).
   _____

Note any challenges that the collaborative group faced and suggest a strategy for improvement.
_____
_____
_____

How can you apply this experience as a fishbowl observer to your own listening and oral communication skills?
_____
_____
_____
_____

IQ: A Practical Guide to Inquiry-based Learning   Reproducibles **149**

FIGURE 25: Reproducible 13

Conversation is key for learning

"The most fruitful and natural exercise for our minds is, in my opinion, conversation."

—Michel de Montaigne

"Learning involves language: the language we use influences learning. On the empirical level researchers have noted that people talk to themselves as they learn. On a more general level there is a collection of arguments, presented most forcefully by Vygotsky, that language and learning are inextricably intertwined."

"Learning is a social activity: our learning is intimately associated with our connection with other human beings, our teachers, our peers, our family as well as casual acquaintances.... We are more likely to be successful in our efforts to educate if we recognize this principle rather than try to avoid it. Much of traditional education, as Dewey pointed out, is directed towards isolating the learner from all social interaction, and towards seeing education as a one-on-one relationship between the learner and the objective material to be learned. In contrast, progressive education...recognizes the social aspect of learning and uses conversation, interaction with others, and the application of knowledge as an integral aspect of learning."

—George E Hein, "Constructivist Learning Theory" (1991)

Q Which ideas presented in the quotes resonate with you?

Q What further questions were provoked by these quotes?

Q What are the challenges in allowing increased levels of social interaction in learning? How do you address these challenges?

Q How have students' experiences in the digital world impacted their social interactions and learning?

Viewing digital and media sources

Our students spend a lot of time outside the classroom exercising their technical skills. The use of the World Wide Web, including its web pages, media, and social networks, is transforming the way we learn and interact with others. Students have developed these skills independently of their schooling. However, in inquiry-based learning classrooms, we must consciously provide opportunities for students to think deeply about how they listen and view complex combinations of text, sound, and visual information.

Two practical ideas for getting students to think critically about the technical sources they use are: 1) asking them view political speeches or commentary or 2) asking them to view or listen to discussions or debates that feature two opposing viewpoints, and to evaluate the communication skills of the speakers.

Speeches, commentary, discussion, and debate can be found on YouTube. Examples of speeches include Stephen Harper's Apology for the Chinese Head Tax or the Residential Schools Apology. Examples of commentary are Rex Murphy's *Point of View* on CBC and comic commentary by Rick Mercer. Examples of discussions and debates include *The Lang & O'Leary Exchange* or panels moderated by TVO's Steve Paikin. Students can use *Reproducible 14: Listening Critically to Media* on p. 150 to practise their listening skills while critically considering oral communication skills and purposes.

REPRODUCIBLE 14: Listening Critically to Media

Name: _____ Date: _____

Topic being discussed: _____

Media source and date: _____

Speech or political commentary

1. Who is the speaker?
2. Who is the intended audience? What is the purpose of the speech/commentary?
3. What is the main idea or argument presented?
4. Describe the speaker's use of voice (tone, pace, pitch, use of pauses).
5. Describe the speaker's use of body language (eye contact, facial expression, body posture).
6. If you were this speaker's oral communication coach, what advice would you give them?

Panel discussion/Debate

1. Who are the speakers?
2. Who is the intended audience? What is the purpose of the panel/debate?
3. What is the main idea or argument presented by each speaker?
4. Choose one speaker and complete the following questions:
   a. Describe the speaker's use of voice (tone, pace, pitch, use of pauses).
   b. Describe the speaker's use of body language (eye contact, facial expression, body posture).
5. Who was the most effective speaker? Consider both the speaker's ideas and their communication skills in your answer.

News report

1. Who is the target audience? What words, sounds, or images suggest this?
2. How many speakers are featured in this report? Are different points of view represented?
3. What part of the story is not being told?
4. Whose point of view carries more weight in the story? How do you know?
5. Consider the impact of visuals and sound effects in persuading and engaging viewers.

150 Reproducibles   *IQ: A Practical Guide to Inquiry-based Learning*

FIGURE 26: **Reproducible 14**

Inquiry journal and conferencing

An **inquiry journal** is a valuable tool to help students practise their written communication skills related to the inquiry process. Consider dividing the journal into sections that represent different inquiry skills (i.e., developing or revising questions, assessing sources, drawing conclusions, and communicating new ideas).

Many of this book's reproducibles for individual tasks could become prompts for a short piece of writing in an inquiry journal. One to three questions or sentence stems can assist students in framing their response and focusing on the necessary skill development. The key in the inquiry journal is quality of written response—not quantity. Teachers should model their own writing of responses, including at the editing stage, and gradually encourage students to do the same.

Writing in the inquiry journal can be assessed by peers. Students should come to see the journal as a valuable record and support of their learning. You may decide that it is best to consider the entries in the journal as part of your triangulated assessment data.

Another important purpose of the inquiry journal is to help represent the student's feelings during an inquiry. We spend a lot of time assessing student's cognitive learning but we have to be equally mindful of their affective learning. A student's emotions and attitudes during the learning process play a role in their engagement, motivation, and willingness to act on feedback and on learning goals. It is not enough that students are given the knowledge and skills to learn; they must also develop the desire to learn. An inquiry classroom (and, by extension, the inquiry journal) is a place where that desire can be nurtured.

Conferences provide time for one-on-one conversations about a student's learning and feelings. Checking in with all students at key stages of the inquiry is an important way to assess for learning. The inquiry journal is the anchor for the conference. Students could decide to highlight parts of their journal in the conference or the teacher could conference with the student, a collaborative pair, or group on specific questions or prompts.

> A student's emotions and attitudes during the learning process play a role in their engagement, motivation, and willingness to act on feedback and on learning goals.

ENSURING SUCCESS

From journal to portfolio

An inquiry journal can easily be extended into an inquiry portfolio by having students select artifacts that represent their best thinking at different stages of the inquiry. An inquiry portfolio can show improvement over time as students complete multiple inquiries.

EXAMPLES

Prompts to develop communication skills specific to an inquiry

- Write a paragraph in which you describe the qualities of a good inquiry question. Provide an example of how you revised a weak inquiry question to a strong inquiry question.

- Submit your point-form notes from one source. Highlight the main arguments presented.

- Create a key visual to show your synthesis of three sources you have assessed.

- Create an information graphic of what you think are the positives and challenges to researching digital sources.

- Write a brief paragraph that summarizes the importance of considering multiple points of view when gathering evidence. Illustrate your paragraph with an example from your research and from classroom conversations in a second paragraph.

- Write a paragraph that clearly demonstrates your understanding of the similarities and differences between ethical and practical considerations in an inquiry.

- Write a persuasive response to the question "Why should I believe your conclusion?"

EXAMPLES

Prompts for self-assessment and self-reflection

- I think I am becoming a better inquiry learner because…

- My goal for improving my listening/collaboration/writing/researching is as follows…

- Here are some strategies I am going to use to reach these goals…

- Here are some ways that other people have stretched my thinking…

- I have a clear idea where I am going in this inquiry because…

- One way the teacher could help me with this learning is…

Prompts for ascertaining student's feelings and attitudes arising from the inquiry

- I am feeling curious/excited/confident/motivated about this part of the inquiry because…

- I am feeling confused/doubtful/frustrated about this part of the inquiry because…

- How can I deal with these feelings in ways that will enhance my success in the inquiry?

Communicating the final product of an inquiry

The final product arising from inquiry provides students with the opportunity to share their thinking with other students and the teacher. To honour the importance of oracy and literacy, it makes sense to have students make an oral presentation and to submit a piece of writing. These final products are introduced to students early on in the inquiry process, since the skills for completing them will be in addition to inquiry skills. Co-constructing success criteria for these final products with your class allows students to have greater ownership and understanding of learning outcomes. Build in sufficient time for rehearsal of oral presentations and editing of written work.

For example, you decide that students should create a photo essay that summarizes their analysis of evidence and their answer to the inquiry question. Therefore, you must spend time considering with students the components of an effective photo essay (i.e., photographs provoke emotional response in addition to providing a specific point of view; written captions summarize for the viewer the perspective and argument being made by the author of the photo essay; paragraphs clearly synthesize analysis of evidence; conclusion is plausible, justifiable, and logical). You would do parallel planning of tasks that focus on inquiry skills along with tasks that require communication and thinking skills to complete an effective product.

In addition to careful planning of the stages leading to the communication of the final product, do consider the fact that technology- and community-based activities will best enable students to apply their learning in real-life contexts that may be relevant and significant to them. It can also be powerful to have parents and community members present at the sharing of final products. In order to increase student comfort with a new type of audience, and to widen the scope of your classroom as a community of inquiry learners, parents, community members, and other colleagues could be included in communicating with students throughout the process. Or they could speak about a question or problem that they have and continue to investigate.

CASE STUDY
Final products

Consider the following case studies of classes working through an inquiry.

- The students in Emma's class are working through an inquiry on whether university or college education should be a human right. This is the last inquiry of the course, and Emma feels that her students have not yet reached their potential as persuasive writers.

- The students in Omri's class are involved in an inquiry regarding the right to digital privacy and how to balance it with security and safety issues. Omri's students are very savvy with technology.

- Rhea's students have been investigating questions related to how to balance conflicting ideas on land use for a specific space in their community. This is the first inquiry that Rhea's students have experienced in the course, and most of the students in the class are in their third or fourth year of English language learning.

Q What final product(s) would you consider as an appropriate and engaging task for students to communicate their overall learning of the inquiry?

Q How do your suggested products balance oracy (speaking and listening) and literacy (written and digital)?

Q How would you integrate tasks into the inquiry process that would allow students to get better at specific communication skills?

Q What criteria would you think are most important in terms of communication for the products that you have suggested?

Q How might you include community-based activities and technology to allow students to apply their learning in real-life contexts?

Q How might you include parents, community members, and other colleagues into the inquiry process and product?

4.3

How can communication be assessed in a final product?

Chapter 2 includes *Reproducible 2: Inquiry Rubric* (p. 138), which could be used as a starting point for co-constructing criteria with your students. Below, the section on communication is reproduced. It is meant as a starting point for planning communication tasks, assessing student growth in communication skills, and (if required) evaluating the communication component of a final product.

Success criteria categories	High degree of effectiveness	Considerable effectiveness	Some effectiveness	Limited effectiveness	Further support required
Communicate new understandings **The student will** communicate clearly					
communicate persuasively					
engage the audience					
use the vocabulary and terminology of the discipline					

FIGURE 27: **Assessing communication in an inquiry**

Barry has decided to have his students create a web quest as the final product of their inquiry, "Is the Canadian justice system just?"

A web quest is a digital representation of an inquiry, where the creator provides key questions, evidence, and interactions to lead the viewer to a possible (or determined) answer. The web quest often includes interactive checkpoints for the viewer to assess his or her understanding of the content presented.

The purpose of a web quest is to present questions and evidence in an engaging and exciting manner. The web-based format is intended to maintain the viewer's interest while increasing knowledge and understanding of the problem presented. The content of the web quest has to be reliable, current, and represent different points of view. Creating a web quest involves high-level digital literacy skills, which some students may demonstrate with ease.

Barry's students have generated their own questions arising from this overarching question and are working together in groups. Examples of some of the group inquiry questions include:

- Are teenage boys treated fairly by the *Young Offenders Act*?

- Do innocent victims of crimes in Canada achieve justice?

- If justice is "blind," why are Aboriginal peoples overrepresented in Canadian jails?

- If you are wrongly convicted, how can justice be served?

- Do we need more laws to prevent cyberbullying?

- Are people with mental health issues treated fairly during sentencing and incarceration?

Using *Reproducible 2: Inquiry Rubric* (p. 138) with an eye to communication criteria specifically, Barry co-constructs the criteria for "What does a great web quest look like?" He suggests to students the attributes of written text, use of visuals and graphics, layout, and navigation as starting point qualities following brainstorming.

Below is what Barry's class produced in answer to the question "What does a great web quest look like?"

A Great Web Quest: Communication Criteria

The text in the web quest has almost no grammatical or spelling mistakes that impede the user from understanding and enjoyment. It has obviously been well-edited. The web quest is exceptionally attractive and has a useable layout. It is easy to locate all important elements. White space and graphics are used effectively to get ideas across. Background colours and font colours are consistent and easy to read, and used to make viewing easier (font size varies for headings, font styles used purposefully and to improve readability). Links are clearly labelled and allow the user to move from page to page without getting lost (easy to navigate). The content of the web quest is interesting to the people for whom it was intended. The web quest uses links, games, questions, and surveys that are appropriate to the intended audience to make it interactive and engaging. The web quest includes the use of vocabulary and concepts that are important to the problem being examined and explains these terms to the viewer.

Since Barry and his students agree on the communication criteria for a "great" web quest, he can later apply qualifiers to describe a "good web quest," a "fair web quest," and "a web quest that needs more work," since all students should be striving for the highest quality from the outset. Barry will also have to co-construct other criteria with his students on content knowledge, thinking and discipline skills, the cognitive level of the tasks, and the application skills. He keeps in mind that the co-constructed criteria may need revision as he and the class learn more about web quests together.

Q What are the benefits of co-constructing success criteria for student learning?

Q What are the possible challenges of co-constructing success criteria with your students? How might you ameliorate possible challenges?

Q Think about an important learning goal in your course and begin to sketch out essential success criteria with your students that will allow them to peer and self-assess.

REVISIT AND REFLECT

This chapter explored how communication defines, sustains, and expands inquiry-based learning. Speaking, listening, and digital literacy skills were at the forefront of this exploration. The genesis of inquiry occurs when one puzzled person articulates an important question to others in the hopes of beginning a meaningful dialogue—to create more understanding or to find solutions to problems.

Students can become better inquiry communicators through the use of classroom and community tasks such as engaging in purposeful dialogue, creating digital communications, reflecting on how to improve listening skills, and using tools such as portfolios and conversation protocols.

To conclude your exploration of this chapter, take some time to think through these questions:

Q What other words would you want to include in an essential inquiry vocabulary list for your class?

Q What terms from the essential inquiry vocabulary list do you think will be most challenging for your students? On a practical level, how could you ensure that students leave your class with a good understanding of these terms?

Q What specific tasks do you plan to use to improve students' listening? How will you assess this task?

Q When you reflect on your classroom, are all communication methods valued equally—in daily work and in evaluated products? Is there any reason to change what you value? Why?

CHAPTER 5
GATHER AND ANALYZE

5.1 What are the key considerations when gathering sources?

5.2 What are some practical strategies for analyzing sources?

What are the key considerations when gathering sources?

A student may have the best inquiry question in the world, but if he or she is not able to gather an array of strong sources, representing a variety of perspectives and points of view, the inquiry will not be successful. This is because the conclusion or response to the inquiry question has to be supported or disproven by information, data, and evidence. If a student does not gather a group of rich sources while working through the inquiry process, then the response to the inquiry question will be an opinion, not critical thinking.

So how do we help our students during the gather-and-analyze stage of an inquiry to ensure their success? We can help them to identify what they think and believe in, and how these orientations influence the gathering stage. We can work within "walled-garden" websites that contain sources for their grade/reading level, or direct them to trusted websites. And finally, we can help them to navigate the over-abundance of information on the Internet.

ENSURING SUCCESS

Adapting the gather stage for your classroom

Students do not have to complete every step of the inquiry process for themselves. Depending on the literacy level of your students, their learning styles, the amount of instructional time available, and your own personal preferences, you may choose to provide students with the source material needed for the investigation. This may be a good choice for you if you are more concerned with how students synthesize and evaluate the source material (see Chapter 6) rather than developing research skills.

Gathering a variety of sources and perspectives

At the most basic level, students engaged in inquiry-based learning should be gathering a variety of sources (e.g., print, web pages, video, academic writings, opinion pieces) that are legitimate—contain factual information supported by experts—and that reflect a range of viewpoints or perspectives. A variety of sources—or different types of sources—ensures that they will not be overlooking any major sources of evidence for their inquiry. Students also need to read and view sources that reflect diverse points of view and perspectives in order to develop a sophisticated understanding of the complexity of the issue under investigation.

Some students will understand these requirements because they will already have been practising them for years. But many students will not arrive in your class with this skill set. They will need you to teach them explicitly that sources contain certain biases or perspectives, that only certain voices tend to be represented in sources—in the mainstream media in particular—and that searching out and considering voices and perspectives that are often overlooked takes effort and persistence.

Identifying personal points of view and beliefs

Students may be more inclined to collect evidence that supports currently held beliefs and dismiss evidence that contradicts these beliefs. As well, personal point of view may impact the types of evidence searches that students choose to conduct. Students may not consider particular search terms if they have not considered the multiple ways that the inquiry question might be answered. And finally, personal point of view may lead students to overlook evidence that contradicts their own beliefs (see *Figure 28: Ways in which point of view can impact the gather stage*).

Asking students to identify point of view does not mean that teachers are aiming to change students' minds on a particular issue. Understanding students' points of view is useful because it allows teachers to better guide students during the gather stage of the inquiry.

> Students may be more inclined to collect evidence that supports currently held beliefs and dismiss evidence that contradicts these beliefs.

ENSURING SUCCESS

Allow time for reflection

Ask students to stop and think about the assumptions and beliefs they bring to any particular topic. You could ask them to write a short inquiry journal entry about those assumptions and beliefs, how they might affect their research, and their responses to the sources that they read.

Do my consumer choices put the environment at risk?	
Point of view	**Possible impacts on the gathering process**
"My parents say that corporations leave a much larger environmental footprint than individuals, so I'd say no." ↔	Student may overlook information that contradicts her currently held belief.
"I read an article that said climate change research is biased, so probably not." ↔	Student may disregard scientific data and evidence during the gather stage.
"I don't think so because we don't have a car. I saw a television show that said that this is the best thing you can do to reduce pollution." ↔	Student may be inclined to draw a conclusion before considering all the evidence.

FIGURE 28: Ways in which point of view can impact the gather stage

Children, adolescents, and adults alike tend to believe they are not biased and do not hold preconceived ideas or beliefs. Of course, all of us are shaped by the opinions and beliefs of our families, our experiences, the communities in which we live, exposure to the media, and the beliefs of the surrounding culture. As a metacognitive exercise, it is helpful to have students write an inquiry journal entry on their personal point of view and beliefs, or complete an organizer, such as *Reproducible 15: Assessing My Point of View of a Topic* on p. 151, to assess their current point of view and beliefs and how they might impact the research process.

ENSURING SUCCESS

Unpacking the term "bias"

The word "bias" tends to hold the following negative connotations:

- If we have a bias, then the bias itself is negative (e.g., she is biased about cats, therefore, she doesn't like cats).

- It is a "bad" thing to have a bias. The assumption behind this notion is that some people are unbiased, or without bias, which is false. All human beings are biased.

A bias is simply a particular tendency or inclination. One can have a positive bias toward school, or a negative one. One can have a positive bias toward strawberries or chocolate, or a negative bias. Although this may seem obvious to us as adults, this may not be the case for your students. Take a moment to unpack the term "bias" so that students can appreciate that having a bias is simply part of having a human outlook.

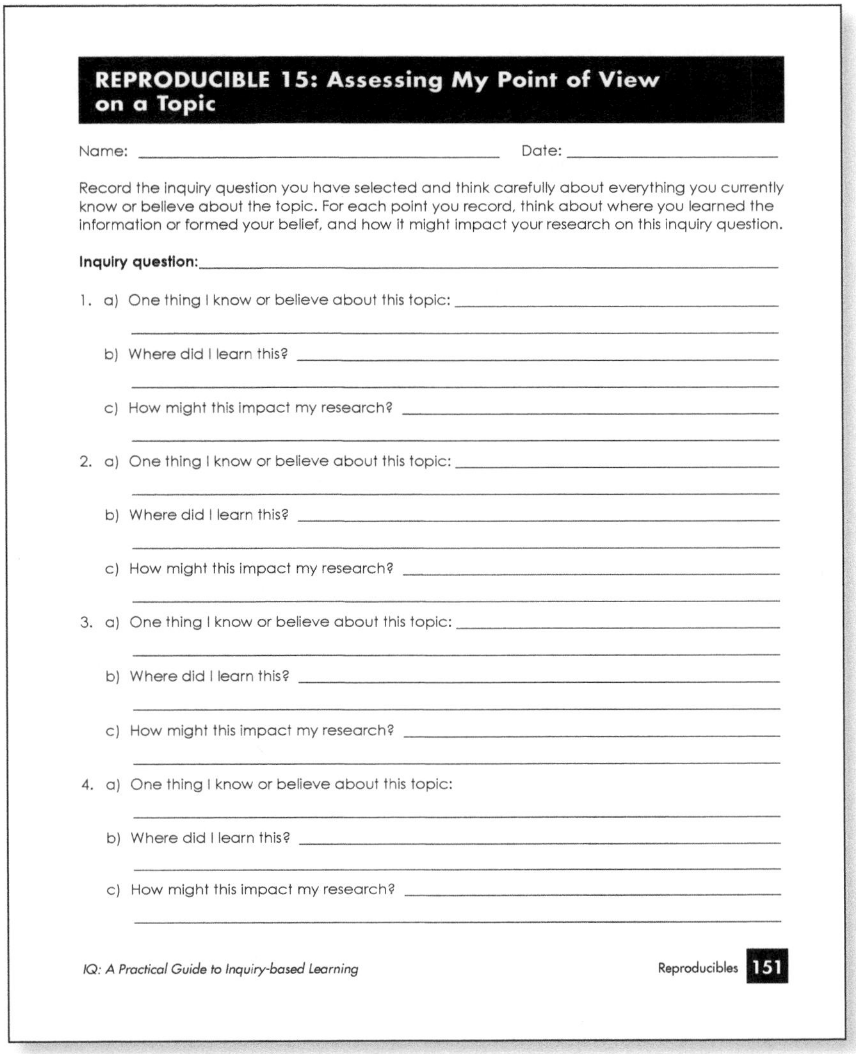

REPRODUCIBLE 15: Assessing My Point of View on a Topic

Name: ______________________ Date: ______________

Record the inquiry question you have selected and think carefully about everything you currently know or believe about the topic. For each point you record, think about where you learned the information or formed your belief, and how it might impact your research on this inquiry question.

Inquiry question: ______________________

1. a) One thing I know or believe about this topic: ______________________

   b) Where did I learn this? ______________________

   c) How might this impact my research? ______________________

2. a) One thing I know or believe about this topic: ______________________

   b) Where did I learn this? ______________________

   c) How might this impact my research? ______________________

3. a) One thing I know or believe about this topic: ______________________

   b) Where did I learn this? ______________________

   c) How might this impact my research? ______________________

4. a) One thing I know or believe about this topic:

   b) Where did I learn this? ______________________

   c) How might this impact my research? ______________________

IQ: A Practical Guide to Inquiry-based Learning Reproducibles 151

FIGURE 29: **Reproducible 15**

Accessing sources that your students can actually read and understand

You probably already know that an inquiry can falter at the gather stage of the inquiry process. There are a few reasons for this. First, research is a complex task which students don't inherently know how to do. Second, teachers have limited time in which to teach this skill.

More important, however, is the fact that it is hard for students to work from sources that are not levelled according to their age, grade, or reading ability. The work of Sam Wineburg, of Stanford University in California, is relevant to this subject. Wineburg has conducted research on the ability of students to read and their ability to think (1991, 2013). His work was done primarily in the area of history and social studies, with students working from primary source documents. His research has highlighted the difference between how "experts" and "novices" tend to read historical texts. *Figure 30* shares some of those differences.

Experts...	Novices...
Ask what the text *does* (purpose).	Ask what the text *says* ("facts").
See texts as a *construction* of a vision of the world.	See texts as a *description* of the world.
See texts as *made by persons with a view of events.*	See texts as *accounts of what really happened.*
Consider *textbooks less trustworthy* than other kinds of documents.	Consider *textbooks very trustworthy* sources.
Assume *bias* in texts.	Assume *neutrality, objectivity* in texts.
Compare texts to judge different, perhaps divergent accounts of the same event or topic.	Use texts to *learn the "right answer."*
Check the *sources* of document.	Read the *document* only.

FIGURE 30: **How experts and novices tend to read historical texts**

SOURCE: Lightfoot, Judy, "Outline of Sam Wineburg's 'On the reading of historical texts,'" http://home.earthlink.net/~judylightfoot/Wineburg.html.

Wineburg's *Reading Like a Historian* (2013) links bundled, levelled, primary sources to American history topics. In fact, Wineburg—one of the most highly respected academics working in the area of historical thinking and critical literacy—believes that it is so important that students can read and understand primary sources that he recommends that primary sources should be altered or edited so that the contents are accessible to readers of different abilities. This idea, presented at the Annual General Meeting of The Historical Thinking Project in Toronto in February 2011, is extremely controversial amongst those people who believe primary sources cannot be modified in any way because then their validity and authenticity are destroyed.

What does Wineburg's research teach us about the gather stage of the inquiry process? It helps us to understand that reading is an incredibly complex skill and that students need help to successfully navigate this part of the inquiry process.

One solution: "walled-garden" websites

These problems may be addressed by working from self-contained websites, also known as "walled-garden" websites. These are websites whose contents have been approved by an authority qualified to

The gather-and-analyze stage

Okay, is there anything about inquiry-based learning we haven't covered?

FIGURE 31: Don't let the gather-and-analyze stage be the elephant in the room

determine the appropriateness of content. Examples include the History Docs developed by the Critical Thinking Consortium in British Columbia and the digital collections of the Saskatchewan Archives. Another example of such a site is the *Canadian Investigations* teaching program created by Oxford University Press Canada.

The *Canadian Investigations* teaching program, created for courses in civics, geography, and history, includes a series of inquiry questions on content topics tied to the Ontario curriculum guidelines (but applicable in other provinces and territories). Each inquiry question—called an "investigation question" in the program—is paired with a series of "source bundles," containing levelled, grade-appropriate primary and secondary sources. The source bundles make it possible for students to consider a variety of quality sources from a range of perspectives, allowing them to explore their inquiry question without wasting time surfing the web or trying to read sources that are above their reading level.

Q&A

Should I differentiate the number of sources required for different levels of learners?

The primary issue is the quality of sources gathered, not the number of sources gathered. One student may have five rich sources that are valid and reliable, reflect a variety of perspectives, and provide evidence to address the inquiry question under investigation. Another student may have 20 sources that do not meet these criteria and therefore are not sufficient. It will take some time for students to understand and accept that it is not the number, but the *quality* of sources that matters regardless of the ability level of the student.

As well, these source bundles remove a large barrier that often prevents teachers from conducting their lessons in an inquiry model—the time that it takes to find appropriate, levelled sources for their students to use that address the inquiry question, or inquiry questions, under investigation. Many teachers report that they are unable to put together source bundles more than once or twice per course.

Finally, the source bundles help to ensure that students will succeed at inquiry-based learning. Nothing makes students give up more quickly than when they are faced with a task they do not believe they can complete. This is not to say that students can't or shouldn't conduct their own additional Internet research to supplement the sources in the bundles, or that class time shouldn't be spent teaching research skills. However, by using source bundles, more class time can be spent on the key inquiry skills of analyzing the sources and assessing the evidence to reach a conclusion or product.

Q&A

How can I help students at lower reading levels gather good evidence?

Students can access information, opinions, data, and other evidence from a variety of sources. Photographs and video clips are authentic sources of evidence. Guide your students to sources in a variety of formats. Reassure your students that these sources of information can be as valid and reliable as traditional print sources.

Example of an inquiry question with accompanying source bundle

"Is illegal action ever justified to bring about a desired change?"

This inquiry question, taken from *Canadian Investigations: Civics and Citizenship* (2014) from Oxford University Press, is accompanied by three source bundles. The bundles include three examples of events or groups that involved illegal action: the Occupy Movement of 2011, the environmental and activist organization Greenpeace, and the Jasmine Revolution of 2010–2011. In the interest of brevity, only the source bundle on Greenpeace will be discussed here.

The source bundle begins with a short introduction to provide some context to the bundle. The bundle contains nine sources in a variety of different formats that represent different perspectives and points of view. The format of the sources ranges from website information to photographs to video clips to news articles and more.

Each source begins with a very short summary to provide context, but without narration. It is important that the sources are not accompanied by narration because the sources need to stand alone as pieces of evidence for students to consider and analyze in relation to the inquiry question. However, the sources are often accompanied by a reading prompt as a literacy aid.

SOURCE BUNDLE: GREENPEACE

Protests can involve anything from occupying a public park to outright terrorism. Greenpeace—an organization of environmental activists—has continually tested the limits of illegal but non-violent action since its beginnings. How illegal is too illegal?

Source 1: Greenpeace explains its tactics [*website synopsis*]

This explanation was written by Greenpeace on its own website to justify its actions. Not all of its actions are illegal, but many of them are. Watch for the reasons Greenpeace gives to justify their actions.

> *Greenpeace works for positive change through action, and our principles inspire us to take action to expose and confront environmental abuse by governments and corporations around the world.*
>
> *Guiding all of our actions, always, is our commitment to nonviolence and personal responsibility. These principles are inspired by the Quaker concept of 'bearing witness', which is about taking action based on conscience. Everyone on every Greenpeace action is trained in the principles of nonviolent direct action (NVDA).*
>
> *Direct action is about physically acting to stop an immediate environmental wrong at the scene of the crime. We act to confront those in positions of power with their responsibility for stopping global environmental abuse. We act to raise the level and quality of public debate. Above all, we act to provoke action from those with the power and responsibility to make change happen.*

Source 2: Boarding an oil rig [*video (length 1:37)*]

This video clip shows a Greenpeace team illegally boarding an oil rig off the coast of Greenland because the oil rig owner, Cairn Energy, had repeatedly refused to produce its oil spill response plan—if it had one. The Greenpeace team shut down oil rig operations for eight hours. As you view this video, consider the action taken by Greenpeace and whether there were any alternatives.

Source 3: Occupying an oil sands pit [*video (length 6:05)*]

In 2009, Greenpeace engaged in three actions designed to briefly shut down a Canadian oil sands operation. As you view this video, think about why an oil company would cease operations while trespassers are on an operation site.

Source 4: Three strategies [*photographs*]

These photographs show three different illegal tactics Greenpeace has engaged in. Read the captions to identify the cause and the illegal action. Would the media be more interested in these photographs or in press releases from Greenpeace?

Ottawa, ON—On the opening day of climate change negotiations in Copenhagen, Greenpeace activists occupy roofs on the Parliament Buildings in Ottawa.

Victoria, BC—Greenpeace activists target Redlist species by chaining freezer doors shut and locking up seafood in shopping carts on the first day of a cross-Canada campaign.

Montreal, QC—Greenpeace activists in Montreal shovel corn into a pile as they demand that GE food be labelled so that consumers know what they are buying.

Source 5: What the law says about Greenpeace tactics [*news article*]

Journalist Jim Bronskill writes about an RCMP report that warns of a "growing radicalized environmentalist faction" and singles out Greenpeace for attention. What does the report say is illegal about Greenpeace tactics? Whose health and safety does it say that Greenpeace puts at risk? A Greenpeace spokesperson says that "There is a difference between breaking the law and criminal activities." Do you agree or not?

> OTTAWA — There is a "growing radicalized environmentalist faction" in Canada that is opposed to the country's energy sector policies, warns a newly declassified intelligence report...

Source 6: The Hewlett-Packard action: What happened?

[*photograph (not shown); web article*]

Hewlett-Packard had delayed implementing a commitment to reduce the hazardous content of its electronic products such as computers, printers, and scanners. Examine the photograph and report from the website TreeHugger to find out what Greenpeace did about it. (TreeHugger is a media outlet dedicated to pushing sustainability into the mainstream.)

Greenpeace Trespasses, Paints on HP's Roof to Protest Hazardous Materials in Electronics Products

Greenpeace is up to their usual antics to try and bring attention to an electronics manufacturer they're particularly upset with — Hewlett-Packard. This morning, Greenpeace activists climbed to the roof of HP's global headquarters in Palo Alto, California and painted "Hazardous Products" in enormous letters. It is a response to the fact that HP is backing away from a promise to exclude PVC and BFRs from their products by the end of the year. But, do big words on a rooftop lead to big actions from big manufacturers? Greenpeace activists painted the message "Hazardous Products" in big, bold letters on the roof as a way to protest the backtracking of the company, and with the hopes that it would get the company to be serious about removing toxic materials from their products.

The message, applied using non toxic children's finger-paint, covered over 11,500 square ft. [1070 square metres], or the size of two and half basketball courts.

Source 7: The Hewlett-Packard Perspective [*excerpt from a statement by HP*]
Hewlett-Packard issued the following response, defending its environmental record, immediately following the Greenpeace action. Watch for words or phrases that might indicate bias.

Hewlett-Packard: In Response to the Greenpeace Attack

The unconstructive antics at HP's headquarters today did nothing to advance the goals that all who care about the environment share. HP will continue its efforts to develop new products and programs around the globe that help the company, its business partners, and customers conserve energy, reduce materials use, and reduce waste through responsible reuse and recycling. HP supports industry efforts to eliminate BFR and PVC because of potential e-waste issues. HP is a worldwide leader in e-waste recycling. HP has recycled 1 billion pounds of electronic products from 1987 to 2007 and has committed to recycling another billion pounds between 2008 and 2011.

Source 8: The Greenpeace Perspective [*web column*]
Mike Gaworecki, web editor for Greenpeace USA, wrote a guest column on the website TreeHugger to defend Greenpeace's illegal tactics. Watch for words or phrases that might indicate bias.

Greenpeace: In Defense of Our Recent Activism Tactics

Greenpeace has been campaigning to get toxic chemicals out of electronics for four years. [...] We met with HP execs, and that got us nowhere. Something had to be done to remind HP of its obligations to be a responsible corporate citizen of the world. So Greenpeace activists did what they do best: they took action. In order to highlight the enormity of the problem, they painted "Hazardous Products" on top of HP's headquarters (in non-toxic, water-soluble paint of course). And now people the world over are discussing HP's business practices.

Source 9: Opinions for and against Greenpeace's HP action

[*comments on a website*]

After Greenpeace's HP action, readers of the TreeHugger website hotly debated whether or not the action was justified. See what just a few of them thought about it. As you read, consider which writer you think is most convincing and why.

> **Guest:** *I hope at the very least that Greenpeace is going to pay to clean up the vandalism. This is not an acceptable method of communication for adults. These are the antics of petulant cause-happy 'rainbow warriors' whose 'important activism' shields them from having to make any useful contribution.*
>
> *I absolutely support removing hazardous materials from consumer products, even at a cost to the company when plausible. However... Greenpeace would be better funding research into alternative safe materials or promoting companies who use such materials (go be all pro-Apple YAY!!) rather then deface the property of a company that is at least making progress.*
>
> **Pieter:** *The response of HP is just a standard PR story from the drawer. There is no explanation or justification why they are backtracking.*
>
> *This kind of pollution affects everybody on this planet, fighting is more important than having a little paint on your roof. So I say: go Greenpeace go!*

A quick examination of the sources in the example bundle indicates that there are an appropriate number of sources providing a variety of source types and different points of view. Students who are sophisticated readers may not select the same sources as students who are less experienced. The variety of perspectives presented also ensures that students will be exposed to different points of view about the inquiry question. Finally, the number of sources allows for an in-depth exploration of the issue without overwhelming students.

Keep in mind that this is just one source bundle linked to the inquiry question. There are many more sources linked to the question under investigation.

Simplifying Internet research

When it comes to gathering sources during an inquiry, the Internet poses both an advantage and a challenge. Unlike previous generations, today's students can access digital information that was previously unavailable, such as museum and archive collections. This opens up a huge range of possible topics and issues for exploration. On the other hand, digital access has also resulted in a deluge of information that is overwhelming for adults, let alone students. Mitchell Kapor states that trying to get information off the Internet is like trying to take a drink from a fire hydrant. In your experience, how do your students respond when they are faced with too much information?

A simple Internet search of the phrase "The October Crisis," for example, nets over 500 million hits. Clearly, it is impossible for students to visit more than a few of those sites. And if they are only going to visit a few, which will they choose? In our experience, students usually click on the first few hits that appear at the top of the search list. They do not have the skills to sift and sort the hits based on the type of source, the purpose of the source, the credibility of the author or publisher, or the point of view of the author or publisher.

"Research is formalized curiosity. It is poking and prying with a purpose."
—Zora Neale Hurston

FIGURE 32: The deluge of information available from the Internet can be overwhelming for students

So how can we help our students to gather good resources from the Internet in an efficient manner? There are three key steps we can take to increase their chances of success.

1. Assist them in developing a specific search focus.

Instead of doing a broad general search, students should try to pursue a *specific search focus* if they are going to work from a search engine online. This involves entering specific key words in addition to the general search term. The addition of a key word or two will dramatically reduce the number of hits that a search produces.

For example, an Internet search of the general phrase "The October Crisis" is too broad and will produce too many results. The example below illustrates how the number of hits reduces with the addition of key words or terms:

- October Crisis = 544 000 000 hits

- October Crisis and the War Measures Act = 1 500 000 hits

- October Crisis and the FLQ = 118 000 hits

- October Crisis and Pierre Laporte = 33 000 hits

Of course, having a specific search focus doesn't mean that students will be finding quality sources, or sources that are at their own reading level, but it will result in them thinking more deeply about their inquiry question and the approach they should take to their research.

2. Direct them to sites you trust.

You can help your students by sending them to specific sites, rather than having them do general Internet searches. Some websites with quality sources that we have found useful are listed in *Reproducible 16: Trustworthy Websites for Gathering Sources* on p. 152. You will likely have your own favoured websites that you would add to this list. You can post this list in your classroom, provide it as a handout, or project it on the screen whenever your students are conducting research.

ENSURING SUCCESS

Modelling inquiry

For the first inquiries in the course, teachers should model the steps of the inquiry process for students. With time, and as students are ready, teachers gradually release responsibility and students start to work more independently. See p. 103 of this chapter for more information on the gradual release of responsibility.

REPRODUCIBLE 16: Trustworthy Websites for Gathering Sources

Name: ______________________________ Date: ____________________

Canadian Museum of Immigration at Pier 21, www.pier21.ca
Primary sources have been bundled on topics that include:

- War Brides
- Jewish War Orphans
- British Evacuee Children
- Immigration

CBC, www.cbc.ca
Current events and in-depth news features can be found on this site. It is a public site and there is no fee or limit on how many articles, videos, or podcasts can be viewed.

CBC Archives, www.cbc.ca/archives
This is an archive of older news clips from television and radio broadcasts. These primary sources capture historical events as they unfolded. The clips are short, so your students will be able to quickly find out if particular clips will help them to address their inquiry question. The information on the website has been organized by general categories (e.g., Environment, Health, Politics, and Economics) and some of it has been organized by more specific topics, called WebQuests (found under "For Teachers"). Some of these WebQuests include:

- The Internment of Ukrainians in Canada
- Counting the Costs (Canada and military conflict)
- Preserving Métis History
- The Mackenzie Valley Pipeline
- Compensation (mercury poisoning in the Grassy Narrows community)

Library and Archives Canada (The Learning Centre), www.collectionscanada.gc.ca/education/008-2010-e.html
The Learning Centre created a list of great sites for both younger children and teenagers that link to many content topics in Canadian classrooms. A sample of topics includes Art, History, Social Studies, Literature, and Science. All of the websites referenced have been vetted as appropriate for young learners, and are age- or grade-appropriate. The only downside to this site is that the Learning Centre is no longer being updated.

Saskatchewan Archives, www.saskarchives.com
Primary sources have been bundled on a variety of Canadian history topics including:

- The Regina Riot
- The Great Depression
- Sod Houses
- Homesteads

152 Reproducibles *IQ: A Practical Guide to Inquiry-based Learning*

FIGURE 33: Reproducible 16

3. Help them to sift through their results.

Students will benefit if you provide them with some key points to help them sift their results. We suggest providing only a few key points, since an exhaustive list will not likely be used by students. As well, conducting an Internet search or two as an entire class via projector will allow you to point out a number of obstacles with Internet research.

a) Consider the author/source, and the date of publication.

Is the author an authority with professional credentials, or someone who is unknown?

- A professional has more credibility—can be more trusted—than someone who is not. You can always do an Internet search for the author to find out if they are well-known and respected in the field they are writing about.

Can you find a date of publication?

- Good sources will always contain publication dates. Those that do not are usually suspect.

b) Be suspicious of websites that have a number of errors.
Errors and blinking emoticons are an indication that the author or organization is not professional. This means you can't really trust the information on the website.

c) Be suspicious of websites that do not list any information about the creator of the site and what would qualify him or her to write about the topic.

d) Check the backlinks (an incoming hyperlink from one website to another) for the website.

Students can find out how many major websites link to, or recommend, the website they are viewing. A website that has a lot of backlinks is usually one that is well-respected by others. Students can check the backlinks in Google by entering "link:<website URL>" in the search field.

These four points could be the basis of fundamental criteria that students use to assess websites. In order to provide descriptive feedback, the teacher, through conversations, observations, or a written product, would determine to what extent the students understand and are using the criteria. When this evidence is gathered, then the teacher can provide descriptive feedback to help students' learning move forward and to help students become independent assessors of their own work (and a peer assessor of other students' work).

EXAMPLE

Ongoing descriptive feedback through conversation

You: *Tell me why this web source you picked is a good one, based on the criteria we have discussed in class.*

Student: *Well, it was published in 2010, so that's pretty recent. There are lots of backlinks to other people's blogs, and the author seems really knowledgeable.*

You: *What else could you have done to make sure the author is knowledgeable on this topic?*

Student: *I could have searched for who they are and what they do—like if they are an expert in the field or something.*

You: *Do you think that backlinks to other people's blogs makes the site credible?*

Student: *Yes.*

You: *Why do you think that?*

Student: *Because a lot of people agree with the information and want to share it.*

You: *Does that fact guarantee that the information is correct and accurate?*

Student: *Maybe not...*

You: *Can you check the backlinks again and see if there are any links to other websites, other than blogs, and get back to me on what you find? Also, do more digging about the author and why they should be trusted as a reliable source of information. Once you have done that and checked back with me, I'd like you to help assess another student's work on assessing websites.*

Student: *Okay then.*

This short example is a model of the importance of criteria, specific and timely feedback, and the movement to student autonomy.

5.2 What are some practical strategies for analyzing sources?

Your students have now gathered a host of sources that they think will help them respond to the inquiry question under investigation. So now what? Students now need to take some time to:

- analyze the sources that they have,
- decide if they've collected a sufficient variety of sources representing a diverse range of perspectives, and
- determine if they need to conduct any further research.

Evaluating evidence

There are many templates on the web to help students analyze sources. Often, however, the templates are accompanied by a long sequence of questions. The sheer number of questions may be overwhelming for students. It is important to remember that we need to chunk each step of the inquiry process in a way that works for students. Since many of our students do not yet have sophisticated research and analysis skills, it is usually preferable to prepare short, concise tasks for students to help ensure their success.

The six questions for evaluating evidence outlined by Peter Seixas and Tom Morton in their 2013 book *The Big Six Historical Thinking Concepts* are a helpful guideline. The questions are simply phrased and therefore accessible to students, and they address each of the crucial points needed for a thorough analysis of the information and data collected. The questions ask students to identify the source itself, to reflect on the objective, usefulness, and reliability of the source, and to consider the context of the source and the evidence it provides. These questions can be found in *Reproducible 17: SOURCE—Evaluating Your Evidence* on p. 153, which you can distribute to students.

FIGURE 34: **Reproducible 17**

Considering a variety of perspectives

Another important consideration involved in the analysis of sources is whether or not a variety of perspectives has been addressed in the sources collected. Students cannot properly address an inquiry question if they have not examined many different perspectives. At the most basic level, that means asking students to categorize their sources according to those that:

- provide evidence and information to support the inquiry question,

- challenge the inquiry question, and

- are neutral and do not clearly either support or challenge the inquiry question.

At a more sophisticated level, it requires students to consider whose voices are included in the collected materials, and whose are left out.

The following set of questions, adapted from the Ontario Ministry of Education's 2012 *Adolescent Literacy Guide*, allow students to dig deeper to consider the variety of perspectives that are addressed in the sources they gathered.

1. What does the author want me to know, think, or feel? How do I know this?
2. What view of the world does this source present? How do I know this?
3. What voices, points of view, and perspectives are missing from this source, or all my sources? How significant is their omission?
4. Is this source fair? Why or why not?

As always, teachers may need to conduct an analysis of a number of sources with the class as a whole in order for students to become comfortable and confident with analyzing sources for bias.

Determining when enough evidence has been collected

During the inquiry, students are likely to ask you if they have collected enough evidence. This is a challenge because it places the onus on you to make this determination, and because the answer to the question can only be "It depends."

When students are new to the inquiry process they will look to you for guidance in determining how they are doing at each stage of the investigation. That is why providing formative assessment feedback is so valuable. Students will know how they are doing and will be able to go back and address anything they have overlooked before they proceed further. As well, formative assessment allows you to know exactly how each student is doing, and when it is time to give a group lesson on a particular task or aspect of the inquiry that needs further clarification.

As students become more familiar, skilled, and confident with inquiry-based learning, their need for feedback will still exist, but they will gradually take on more responsibility for their learning and will not need to check in with you as often. This process—referred to as a gradual release of responsibility—is outlined in *Figure 35*.

Although students will want you to tell them the actual number of sources they need to collect in the gather phase of the inquiry, it will be hard for you to give them such a number because it really depends on what they found. You will need to remind them that after they have analyzed their sources (using the six questions outlined in *Reproducible 17*, for example) they need to determine if:

Demonstration
- Teacher models, explains, demonstrates, and thinks aloud

Shared demonstration
- Teacher instructs and teacher and students practise together

Guided practice
- Students practise and teacher coaches

Independent practice
- Students practise on their own and teacher gives feedback

FIGURE 35: Gradual release of responsibility

- the sources they've located are reliable and valid,
- they provide the evidence they need to address the inquiry question, and
- they represent a sufficient number of perspectives.

Their research at this phase is complete only when they can answer yes to these points.

In addition, if they do have a substantial number of rich, high-quality sources from a variety of perspectives but they do not have enough evidence to respond to the inquiry question, then it may be time for them to revisit their inquiry question and revise it in some way. They may need to simply tweak their inquiry question, or they may realize that the evidence they've found points them in a new direction.

ENSURING SUCCESS

Assessing your students' ability to analyze sources

Earlier in this chapter we discussed six good questions that students should ask when analyzing sources:

- ☑ Where did it come from?
- ☑ For what purpose was it created?
- ☑ Is it relevant to the inquiry question under investigation?
- ☑ Is it accurate, unbiased, and reliable?
- ☑ Is it supported by other evidence?
- ☑ What does it prove?

Post these six questions prominently in your room, or give students Reproducible 17: SOURCE—Evaluating Your Evidence to keep in their notebooks. In addition to encouraging students to use the questions any time they are working from sources, also allow students to use the handout or posters during formal tests. Remember that you want to assess their ability to analyze sources, not their ability to memorize the six questions. The questions are a tool that will ensure their success.

Determining when enough evidence has been collected

Farah and Mia are working together on the inquiry question "Is illegal action ever justified to bring about change?" They have selected many of the source materials from the three *Canadian Investigations* source bundles linked to this inquiry. They have also conducted additional Internet research during class time.

When they were gathering their sources they took the time to evaluate each one according to each of the six SOURCE criteria:

☑ Where did it come from?

☑ For what purpose was it created?

☑ Is it relevant to the inquiry question under investigation?

☑ Is it accurate, unbiased, and reliable?

☑ Is it supported by other evidence?

☑ What does it prove?

At this stage in the inquiry process, the girls have to stop and analyze the sources they have gathered to determine whether they have collected enough evidence to proceed to the next step of the inquiry. The teacher has modelled this exercise with the class as a whole group. This is the first time the girls have tried to do this task independently.

FARAH: *Okay, so our inquiry question—"Is illegal action ever justified to bring about change?"—can probably be answered in three ways, right? Yes, No, It Depends.*

MIA: *Right. And I guess the answer depends on what we find in the evidence. So let's see what we have collected so far.*

FARAH: *Sure. We've already gotten rid of evidence that we didn't think was any good, because it didn't meet the SOURCE criteria.*

MIA: *Yes. We just have to figure out if we gathered enough evidence from a variety of perspectives and that type of thing, so we know whether we can move on to the next step. And we have this organizer from the teacher to help us with this part.*

After the girls entered the source information into the chart (provided as *Reproducible 18: Gather Stage—Determining When You Have Enough Evidence* on p. 154) they found that they had 12 good sources altogether. Seven of the sources provided some evidence that illegal action is sometimes justified to bring about change. Four sources did not support this premise. One source was inconclusive.

REPRODUCIBLE 18: Gather Stage—Determining When You Have Enough Evidence

Name: _____   Date: _____

Use this template to assess whether you have enough evidence to start answering your inquiry question.

Inquiry question: _____

Source	Support	Challenge	Both

Do you have sources that represent a variety of perspectives and points of view on the inquiry question?

FIGURE 36: **Reproducible 18**

The sources represented a variety of perspectives and points of view, so at this point they felt they had a sufficient number of sources gathered and decided that no further research was required.

Q Having students work together at times during an inquiry can increase the chances that they will proceed smoothly through each step of the inquiry process. In this case study, the girls worked together on the gather-and-analyze stage. What other stages of the inquiry process do you feel would work best if completed in pairs or within a small group?

REVISIT AND REFLECT

This chapter explored the gather-and-analyze stage of the inquiry process. Students need to ensure that they collect a variety of sources that include a variety of perspectives and they must be aware how their own points of view and beliefs can affect the research process. In addition, the chapter discussed the importance of having students work with sources at an appropriate reading level, and how "walled-garden" websites can help to facilitate the process. We acknowledged the difficulties students encounter when conducting research on the Internet, as well as what we can do in classrooms to simplify the Internet research process for students.

As students gather their evidence during the inquiry process, they also have to analyze the materials they are gathering. It is possible to spend weeks and weeks gathering research, but that is neither feasible nor advisable. Any task that doesn't have clear parameters will quickly cause students to shut down or, at the very least, reduce their level of engagement. It can help to keep students focused when they are gathering evidence if they are analyzing the quality of the source material and ensuring that they are gathering material that represents a variety of perspectives. This also allows them to determine when they have gathered enough evidence to proceed to the next stage of the inquiry process.

To conclude your exploration of this chapter, take some time to think through these questions:

Q What are the challenges you face personally when trying to guide students through a project that has a research component?

Q How do your students respond to the idea of conducting research? Is it a task that they welcome or one they dread?

Q How much time do you spend explicitly teaching Internet research strategies? What strategies other than those outlined in this chapter would you recommend?

Q Under what conditions might you consider providing students with the source material they need for their inquiry, rather than having them conduct this step in the inquiry process themselves?

CHAPTER 6
SYNTHESIZE, EVALUATE, AND DRAW CONCLUSIONS

6.1 How can I help my students make sense of their evidence and data?

6.2 How should students use evidence and data to evaluate and draw conclusions?

6.1

How can I help my students make sense of their evidence and data?

Most students are challenged by the task of making sense of evidence and data. It is one thing for a student to be able to read or view a piece of evidence and understand it, but it takes an entirely different set of skills to be able to determine what the source says about the inquiry question, synthesize all of the source material, evaluate that material, and make a sound conclusion. Some teachers feel that these skills are particularly challenging—if not impossible—for many students to master. But these skills can be taught, and if we allow students multiple opportunities to practise these skills, they can become proficient at all of them.

In this chapter, we will explore the steps you can take to enable students to learn how to synthesize, evaluate, and draw conclusions from their evidence and data. Students with a broad range of academic and language abilities can work with these high-level skills if we provide some very basic tools to assist them. Some of these tools include basic mind maps and PMI (Plus, Minus, Interesting) charts. In the end, this stage of the inquiry process allows students to make new learnings and understandings based on the evidence they have gathered during the inquiry.

"Creative synthesis refers to the mixture of many concepts, visuals, or correlations into a new whole, particularly whenever this varies fundamentally from any of its parts."
—psychology dictionary.org

Synthesizing evidence and information

Once students have gathered good evidence as part of their investigation, they need to synthesize that evidence and information. To *synthesize* is to weave themes and ideas together to create a cohesive picture or line of thought. In a process not unlike jigsaw puzzling, students arrange and rearrange the information fragments until patterns and some kind of picture begins to emerge (see *Figure 37*). For many students, weaving ideas together is the most difficult stage. In many cases, students are running out of time as they try to complete their inquiry. Rather than weaving a fine fabric, they create a quilt of unrelated pieces of information. Students need strategies for analyzing and synthesizing the information they have collected.

FIGURE 37: Students need strategies for analyzing and synthesizing the information they have collected

It is important to remember that our target audience is school-aged children. We need to try to make this stage of the inquiry process engaging and interesting, rather than onerous. To that end, our focus is not on sophisticated researchers who are ready for post-secondary study, but rather, on the typical students that populate our classrooms.

ENSURING SUCCESS

Give your students (and yourself) the gift of time

As teachers, we have all kinds of pressures to meet timelines and deadlines. We have reporting deadlines, curriculum requirements, and may have to proceed through the curriculum in a lock-step fashion with other teachers of the same course. But when we worry too much about moving along according to a schedule, we take away the opportunity for students to engage in rich, deep thinking.

The inquiry process can be thought of as a "brake" because it affords students frequent opportunities to reflect on their learning and loop back to reconsider, revise, and restructure their thoughts. Reducing the volume of tasks and providing more time for reflection increases the chances that students will not only come to understand more about the world, but also about themselves as thinkers and learners.

Identifying trends or patterns in evidence and information

One way for students to synthesize their evidence and information is to identify patterns or trends in the information they have located. Patterns or trends are ideas, themes, or arguments that repeat throughout the evidence. Students can be prompted to identify patterns and trends through questions like the following:

- What is similar about this evidence?

- Are there two or three points or arguments that are consistent across a number of pieces of evidence?

- Does a timeline of the evidence show that people are more concerned about this issue or less concerned about this issue than in the past?

- What does a growing or declining trend tell me about the issue under investigation?

- Is the theme reflected in more than one data source?

- Are smaller patterns contained within the themes? If so, what are they?

- On closer inspection, what evidence is not a good fit? Why?

SOURCE: The last four questions were taken from Donohoo, Jenni, *Collaborative Inquiry for Educators. A Facilitator's Guide to School Improvement*, California: Corwin (2013).

My students often expect me to provide an answer for them rather than coming up with the answers for themselves. How much direction should I provide to students as they try to synthesize the evidence they have collected?

It is true that most students still think that teachers usually ask questions for which there is only one correct answer. Some students in your class may be confident to explore an inquiry question without worrying about finding a "right" answer. But others will be unsure about their own abilities to compose a good, structured response to an inquiry.

You can help students who require more direction by asking them additional questions. Australian educator Kath Murdoch (2012) suggests using the following questions as prompts:

- What will we need to think about before we get started on this?

- How are your ideas about this changing?

- What has been the thing that has most changed your thinking? Why?

- What are you noticing about your thinking?

- How are you feeling about what you have learned/done so far?

Students can be asked to write their ideas and reflect on their learning. This is helpful not only for students, but also for teachers who need to coach and monitor progress. Templates can help students to make visual connections between the pieces of evidence they locate. Mind maps can be a very effective tool for this. When using a mind map, students place the question they are investigating in the centre of the map, and the supporting information in various places around the map according to headings they have assigned. In *Figure 38: Mind map on the historical significance of Vimy Ridge*, the inquiry question has been placed in the centre of the mind map and the evidence is organized around the investigation according to patterns and trends. In addition to traditional pen-and-paper mind maps, students can also create electronic mind maps using Smart Ideas concept-mapping software or Web 2.0 programs (bubbl.us, Mindomo.com).

Making mind maps work for your students

Many students and teachers have experience working with mind maps. Students should know that they should start at the centre of the map and work out. They should also know that they should keep any text on

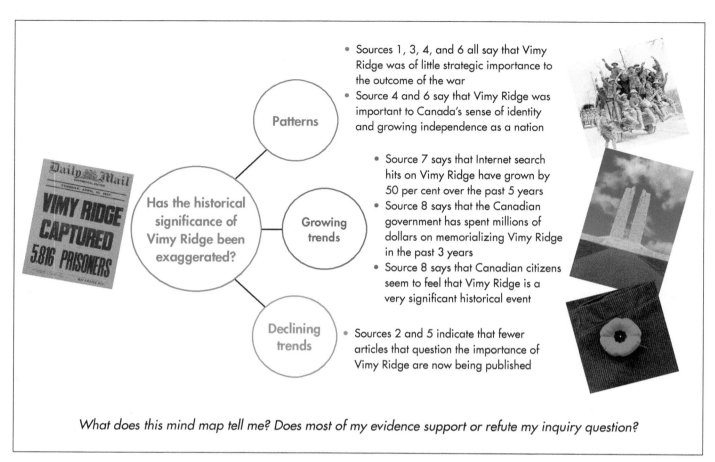

Patterns

- Sources 1, 3, 4, and 6 all say that Vimy Ridge was of little strategic importance to the outcome of the war
- Source 4 and 6 say that Vimy Ridge was important to Canada's sense of identity and growing independence as a nation

Has the historical significance of Vimy Ridge been exaggerated?

Growing trends

- Source 7 says that Internet search hits on Vimy Ridge have grown by 50 per cent over the past 5 years
- Source 8 says that the Canadian government has spent millions of dollars on memorializing Vimy Ridge in the past 3 years
- Source 8 says that Canadian citizens seem to feel that Vimy Ridge is a very significant historical event

Declining trends

- Sources 2 and 5 indicate that fewer articles that question the importance of Vimy Ridge are now being published

What does this mind map tell me? Does most of my evidence support or refute my inquiry question?

FIGURE 38: Mind map on the historical significance of Vimy Ridge

the map neat and readable, and limit the information on the map to key words, images, and visual aids like arrow or icons.

However, like all tools, mind maps can be used in a sophisticated manner with just a few adjustments in the way you present them. The following tips can help you and your students make the greatest use out of mind maps:

☑ Put key words on connecting lines on the mind map. This reinforces the connections students are making.

☑ Use colour to identify patterns and themes.

☑ Encourage your students to include three-dimensional elements on their map. Again, this reinforces patterns and trends.

☑ Think outside the box. If students run out of space, paste more paper onto the map. This will create a more visually-appealing map, and again, it will make patterns and trends obvious.

Making connections between ideas

In addition to looking for patterns and trends when synthesizing information, students can also look for connections between ideas. This can be the connection between their *own* ideas, or connections between the ideas *expressed in the evidence* they have collected.

Let's examine the previous inquiry question, "Has the historical significance of Vimy Ridge been exaggerated?" Students can first look for connections between the personal points of view and beliefs they held about the topic before they began their research and what they have found in the evidence:

Inquiry question: Has the historical significance of Vimy Ridge been exaggerated?	
Personal points of view and beliefs	**Ideas in the evidence**
1. Vimy Ridge must have great historical significance because we spent a great deal of time on it in history class. (Clearly the teacher thinks it was significant.)	1. Sources 5, 7, and 8 say Vimy Ridge was of great military significance.
2. My parents went to France on a trip and made a point of going to Vimy Ridge. (So they must think it was significant.)	
3. I know I've seen commercials on television that say Vimy Ridge was the "birth of the nation."	2. Sources 4 and 6 talk about Vimy Ridge and the birth of the nation.
4. I think any battle where Canadians were killed should be considered to be significant.	3. Sources 1, 3, 4, and 6 say Vimy Ridge was not militarily significant.
My initial position was "Yes."	**The research is pretty evenly split on its significance.**

FIGURE 39: Making connections between personal ideas and evidence

At this point, students would be asked to stop and consider how their personal points of view and beliefs link to the evidence they have gathered. Did the evidence support their initial position or not? If not, why not? If so, how so? As well, they should be challenged to examine whether their personal points of view and beliefs have impacted their selection or their reading of the evidence. If they believe it has, then they should re-read and reconsider the sources they have, and perhaps gather additional resources.

What happens if students begin to synthesize their evidence and then realize that they can't make a cohesive argument in response to the inquiry question? Hasn't the time for them to conduct further research passed? And if not, how am I going to manage a classroom of students all working at different rates and on different phases of their inquiry?

Inquiry does involve and require reflection on the learning as it is taking place. It may happen that students realize that they can't produce a structured response to the inquiry question and need to gather more evidence and data. They may even need to reframe the inquiry question itself.

It is true that when students loop around to another stage in the inquiry process, that other groups will be moving on to their evaluations and conclusions. However, this does not mean that they will be starting their research from scratch. They may only need a few additional pieces of data, and they will already have gained some research skills. They will also be very familiar with the inquiry question, so they will be able to gather resources more quickly than they did the first time.

Although it may feel daunting to have different groups of students working at different stages of the inquiry, this is how most classrooms operate in general. Usually when we assign tasks during class time, some students or groups complete the work quickly and you must decide what to do with those students while the others continue to work. The advantage of the inquiry model is that there are other stages that students can move to as part of the process. For example, some groups may begin to complete their evaluation and conclusions, while others may start to develop their final product.

ENSURING SUCCESS

What does synthesis feel like?

Educator Jamie McKenzie (1999) uses the terms "juxtaposition," "cognitive dissonance," and "resonance" to describe the synthesis stage of the inquiry process. A good inquiry question sets up juxtaposition between ideas and thoughts. The more acute this juxtaposition, the more cognitive dissonance is created. This cognitive dissonance sets off vibration, conflict, and discomfort—in short, students are thrown off balance. Their minds are intrigued, their curiosities are awakened, and they want to bring things back into harmony or resonance.

6.2

How should students use evidence and data to evaluate and draw conclusions?

At this stage of the inquiry process, students determine the implications of their findings. What does the evidence tell them about the question under investigation? What are the big ideas that have been learned? What conclusions can be drawn at this point in the inquiry? The following case study provides an example of this phase of the inquiry process.

CASE STUDY

Reflecting on the question under investigation

When Jack and Sam began working on the inquiry question "What can and should be done when the justice system fails?" they explored their prior assumptions and beliefs and determined that even though they believed the justice system in Canada works well in many cases, there are situations where serious injustice occurs. They weren't sure what they thought should be done about this, but they considered approaching the topic along three different avenues:

- Exploring cases of people who have been wrongly convicted

- Exploring what happens to innocent victims of crime

- Exploring what happens when laws are not enough to stop criminal behaviour

After some preliminary investigation, they decided to focus on the cases of people who have been wrongly convicted. To keep their investigation manageable, they narrowed their research focus to include only Steven Truscott, Donald Marshall, and David Milgaard. As they were gathering evidence, they became familiar with the work of the Association in Defence of the Wrongly Convicted (AIDWYC) and decided that information about this organization should also be included in their investigation.

continued

JACK: Okay, so we decided to focus on Truscott, Marshall, and Milgaard and we had no trouble finding good source material on these three cases.

SAM: Yes, they were good choices because all three of them were later exonerated for the crimes. I think we would have gotten stuck if we had been exploring cases where there was some question as to whether or not they were innocent.

JACK: That's right. Then while we were synthesizing our information, we realized that there were actually two parts to the inquiry question: 1) "What can be done?" and 2) "What should be done?" We decided that "what can be done" must refer to the actual legal steps that can be taken, or rights that people have, if they are wrongly convicted. And we figured that "what should be done" must refer to what we think is the right thing to do for people like them.

SAM: Yeah, and we have to make sure we consider different perspectives and points of view on what should be done with people that are falsely accused. I already noticed in the sources that some people argue that Donald Marshall doesn't deserve anything because he had a long history of criminal behaviour and has therefore cost the criminal justice system all kinds of money.

JACK: Yes, we have to make sure we touch on various opinions and viewpoints. And then we have to wrap up with some overall conclusion or recommendations that answer the inquiry question. Let's use the organizer that the teacher gave us:

Inquiry question: What can and should be done when the justice system fails?			
Content focus of our investigation: Those who have been wrongly convicted and incarcerated			
Evidence in support of argument 1:	**Evidence in support of argument 2:**	**Evidence in support of argument 3:**	**Evidence in support of argument 4:**
Sources that argue for restitution	Sources that argue for public apology	Sources that argue nothing should be done	Other arguments
Our overall conclusion: Additional thoughts/recommendations:			

FIGURE 40: Evaluating and drawing conclusions—Reflecting on the inquiry question

A blank table has been provided as *Reproducible 19* on p. 155.

Q How might you redirect students if they came to you with a conclusion that doesn't seem supported by the evidence?

Q If the evidence found by students is evenly split across two main arguments, how might you help them decide which argument to support?

Q Some classroom teachers have students record themselves talking aloud as they synthesize their data. The recording can then be reviewed by the teacher to better understand the thought process used by the students. Do you think this would be a useful tool for you? Why or why not?

Ensuring success through metacognition

Provide frequent opportunities for students to stop and reflect on their learning. Prompt them in their reflections with questions like the following:

- *"I used to think...but now I am thinking..."*
- *"I had a hunch that...and it looks like I was on the right track because..."*

- *"Here's what I am thinking so far..."*
- *"This conclusion is very different from what I thought it was going to be because..."*

Of course, these questions could be used at any time during the inquiry process, not just during the synthesize stage.

Reflecting on the big ideas being learned

We want our students to leave our classrooms with a deep understanding of the big ideas that underpin the course. Also called *enduring understandings*, the big ideas for any course repeat themselves over and over across units. Big ideas are concepts rather than content. The following big ideas for history, social studies, geography, and civics are provided to help you think about the big ideas that underpin these disciplines. As you read them, you might want to think about the content you teach that aligns with each big idea.

> "An idea is 'big' if it helps us make sense of lots of confusing experiences and seemingly isolated facts. It's like the picture that connects the dots or a simple rule of thumb in a complex field."
>
> —Grant Wiggins (2010)

EXAMPLES

Big ideas in history and social studies

- Decisions have both intended and unintended consequences.
- Those who have power do not give it up easily.
- Determinations of historical significance vary from group to group.
- Decisions to go to war are made by people with power. Those who fight in wars have little power.

EXAMPLES

Big ideas in geography

- Everything has a geography.
- The physical environment affects how we live.
- People disagree about resource ownership, use, and development.
- Communities can be sustainable.

Big ideas in civics

- Rights must be respected for the common good.
- Ideas about citizenship change over time.
- Competing rights must be balanced.
- Inaction has consequences.

If you look through your course outline, which is most likely organized by unit or topic, you will see that these big ideas are actually addressed at a number of points throughout your course. That is because they are the big ideas that underpin the discipline.

Q&A

I've been hearing about "big ideas" for years, but I don't know what the big ideas are for my discipline. Am I failing as a teacher if I don't know what they are, and therefore don't teach them explicitly?

No, you are not failing as a teacher if you do not teach big ideas explicitly. With the proper amount of planning time and a supportive group of colleagues, you'd likely be able to identify them together, but we often don't have this luxury. Many provincial curricula now state the big ideas for each discipline or course, so this can be a great starting point if you've not had a chance to develop a list of big ideas for yourself, or in collaboration with your colleagues.

You don't have to teach everything at once. That is, you don't have to state or teach the big ideas before the students begin an inquiry. You may choose to have your students complete an inquiry and share the results of the inquiry with the class. After all students have shared, this might be a good time to co-construct a few of the big ideas that seemed to repeat across the student responses. As you identify the big ideas, you can post them around your classroom.

Let's return to the inquiry question being explored by Jack and Sam in the case study on pp. 115–116. The question was "What can and should be done when the justice system fails?" They decided to explore this question by studying the cases of three Canadians who were wrongly convicted of murder and then later exonerated. After Jack and Sam have completed their inquiry, they will have learned and will likely remember some of the details of the cases of Truscott, Marshall, and Milgaard. The information they remember will likely include those details they found most interesting and/or horrifying.

However, it is the big ideas that underpin all three cases, rather than the details of the cases themselves, that will comprise the enduring understandings for the inquiry. The big ideas for this inquiry question may include:

- Every Canadian is entitled to fundamental justice.
- Implementing justice requires laws, institutions, and procedures.
- Ideas about justice change.
- Justice systems sometimes fail.

If Jack and Sam leave with these big understandings, they will have done some deep, critical thinking that will continue to affect the way they view crime and justice and what they learn in the future.

Drawing conclusions about the inquiry question based on the evidence

Some students will struggle when trying to conclude their inquiry. This may be because they haven't had experience drawing their own conclusions, they may not feel confident in their critical thinking abilities, or because drawing a conclusion is a higher-order critical thinking skill that they haven't learned yet. But at the most basic level, drawing a conclusion is really about weighing the pros and cons of an issue. If you have students who are struggling with their conclusion(s), it might be helpful for them to complete a basic PMI chart or activity about each of the options under investigation.

The PMI (Plus, Minus, Interesting) chart was developed by Edward de Bono—a physician, author, and consultant—in 1982. De Bono was an early proponent of the deliberate teaching of thinking in schools. The PMI chart has many applications, but it was designed to be a quick tool (three to five minutes in length) to weigh the pros and cons of an issue, to widen the perception of a problem or decision, or to uncover issues that might have been overlooked. In this case, teachers would suggest the use of a PMI chart to help students draw or develop their conclusions. A blank template is provided as *Reproducible 20* on p. 156, but a simple Internet search will provide you with a number of formats to choose from.

Q&A

I find that many students believe there is a "right" answer. How can I reassure them that when conducting an inquiry there really is no "right" answer I want them to find?

An inquiry really is an exploration. When the inquiry begins, the students and teacher do not know exactly what the answer to the inquiry question will be. This is a good thing, but it breaks from a traditional learning model where students "find" the correct answer in a textbook or while watching a film. It will take some time for students to become familiar with inquiry-based learning, and to trust that it is okay for them to truly explore the resources and develop their own structured response to an inquiry question. Of course, some answers are better than others because student responses need to be based on valid evidence.

In the case of Jack and Sam, who were exploring the inquiry question "What can and should be done when the justice system fails?" two PMI charts could be used: one for what *can* be done, and one for what *should* be done. When the boys look at the completed PMI charts, the plus side would provide them with a quick summary of what can and should be done, which they could turn into their conclusion.

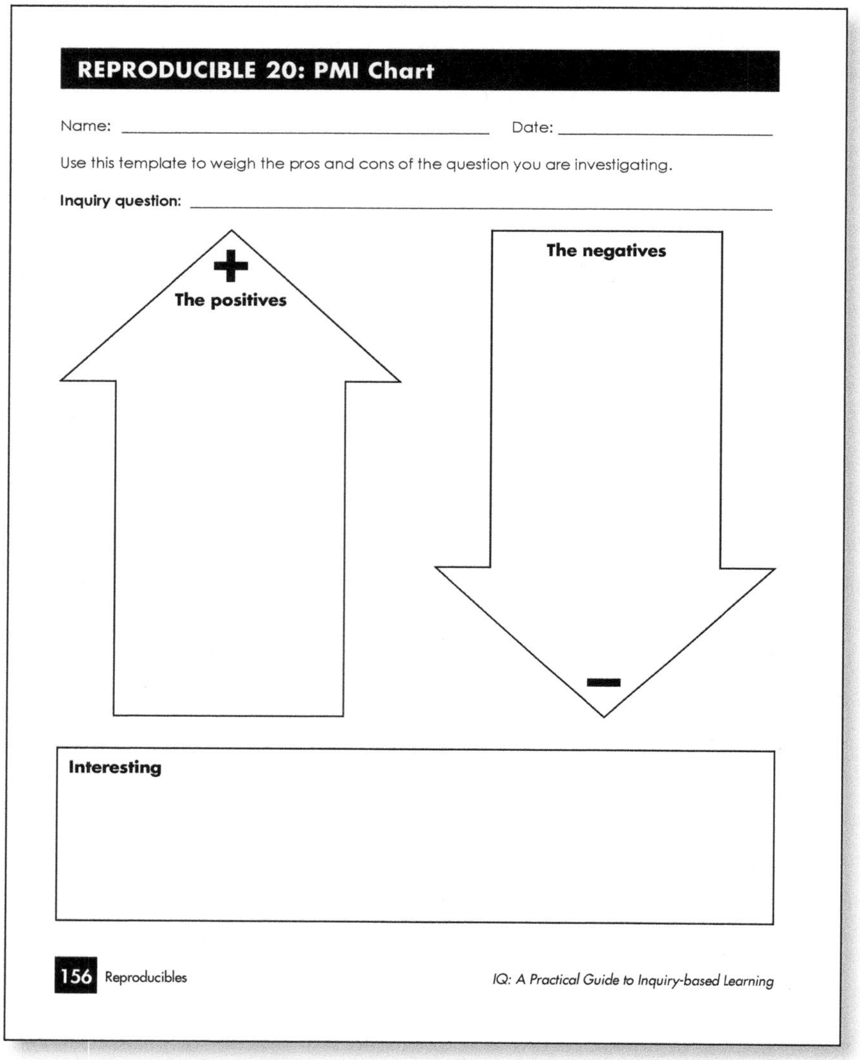

REPRODUCIBLE 20: PMI Chart

Name: ______________________ Date: ______________

Use this template to weigh the pros and cons of the question you are investigating.

Inquiry question: ______________________________

+
The positives
The negatives
–
Interesting

156 Reproducibles

IQ: A Practical Guide to Inquiry-based Learning

FIGURE 41: **Reproducible 20**

One of the goals of inquiry is for students to understand that the conclusions they make about the inquiry question are based on the evidence they find, the prior assumptions they held, and the connections they were able to make between the various pieces of information they studied. Another student working from a different group of sources might come up with an entirely different conclusion. This is a positive result in that it shows how the "answer"—the result of the inquiry—is dependent on a number of factors and that everyone does not need to come to the same conclusion for a given question.

If this situation occurs in your classroom, it can result in a very rich learning experience. As students' findings are shared with one another and the class, these differences provide additional avenues for questioning, considering, and deep thinking.

Q&A

What if after all that time and work, the students do a bad job on the inquiry?

For students with greater literacy challenges, more scaffolding will be necessary to ensure they experience success, but it is unlikely that students will do a bad job on an inquiry. This is because there are a number of checks and balances built into the inquiry process—more than there are in a traditional, Socratic classroom. In Chapter 2, we explored the assessment of inquiry and stressed the fact that assessment should be frequent and ongoing during the inquiry process. This type of assessment allows students to see how they are doing, rethink what they are doing, and improve the direction of the inquiry.

Furthermore, the inquiry process encourages students to frequently pause their work and think about what they are doing, how they are doing, and what they are learning. This metacognition and communication of the learning process allows them to self-correct, peer correct, or come to you with questions and wonderings.

And finally, in an instructional model built around inquiry, students are much more responsible for their learning than in a traditional classroom. They select or create an inquiry question based on their own interests; they are required to gather evidence and data of high quality, representing multiple perspectives and points of view; they have to synthesize their evidence into a structured argument; and arrive at a plausible and well-founded conclusion.

In our experience, all of these elements result in a much higher chance of success, rather than failure.

REVISIT AND REFLECT

This chapter explored the stage of the inquiry process that requires students to synthesize, evaluate, and draw conclusions. For some students this is the most challenging aspect of the inquiry process because it requires them to make connections and look for patterns within information. It involves new and original thinking to make something that is not simply the sum of its parts. Students of differing language levels and with a wide range of academic abilities do have the ability to do this higher-order thinking. Some tried and trusted tools used in other classroom situations, such as mind maps and PMI charts, can help to facilitate this thinking.

This stage of the inquiry process is in many ways the most creative one. Students take everything they have found and learned and construct an argument in response to the inquiry question that is entirely their own. They create something new out of many disparate pieces. These are powerful skills that students can transfer to any subject discipline or learning environment.

To conclude your exploration of this chapter, take some time to think through these questions:

Q What effective teaching strategies do you already use that you could adapt to assist students through this stage of the inquiry process?

Q If your students improved their skills for identifying patterns and trends in information, how might that skill help them in other areas of your course? Or in other courses you teach?

Q If you tried to identify three or four big ideas for each unit of study in your course, what might they be? Would they apply to other courses within your discipline?

Q How do you currently manage your classroom to allow for the different speeds with which your students complete tasks? Which of these classroom management techniques would be useful in an inquiry model of instruction?

CHAPTER 7
IN CLOSING

7.1 Ten key points

IQ: A Practical Guide to Inquiry-based Learning has argued that inquiry-based learning can help to reignite the curiosity and passion for learning that students often seem to lose at school. Inquiry-based learning has a long and honoured history in education—it is not new, even though it seems to be gaining attention with recent changes to curriculum guidelines or directives from school boards.

So if inquiry-based learning is an established instructional approach that engages students, allows them to develop important critical thinking skills, and solves many of the challenges we face in traditional teacher-focused classrooms, why isn't everyone doing it? We believe the answer lies in the lack of practical professional development, resources, and training for classroom teachers.

FIGURE 42: Inquiry-based learning can help reignite curiosity and a passion for learning in your students

You already know that the life of a classroom teacher is an extremely busy one. You must prepare lessons, differentiate for the needs of your students, and conduct ongoing assessment for both student feedback and reporting purposes. And you must do all of this while managing multiple educational initiatives, such as equity, financial literacy, and new assessment requirements. On a daily basis, you face the challenges and opportunities of a diverse student body with a wide range of language and learning needs—not to mention the normal adolescent traits that may make students more interested in talking to their friends than attending to the lesson you are trying to deliver.

However, the same realities and challenges that make it difficult for us to employ new instructional strategies are also the reasons why it is important to do so. Most of us are very pleased with some aspects of the way we run our classrooms, but we all know that there are certain students we are not reaching, or certain components of our courses that are not as effective as we would like them to be. We would all like to find a way to work smarter, not harder.

IQ: A Practical Guide to Inquiry-based Learning has identified the qualities of a successful inquiry program and practical suggestions for planning, teaching, and assessment. To conclude this book, we offer ten key points of inquiry-based learning that are fundamental to classroom success.

> **The same realities and challenges that make it difficult for us to employ new instructional strategies are also the reasons why it is important to do so.**

1. Decide on the type of inquiry that will work best for you

When conducting an inquiry for the first time, it is best to plan for a *guided* inquiry. In a guided inquiry, you assist your students throughout the process by selecting the question, providing specific frameworks and resources in the investigation, and modelling each step of the inquiry process. You may also choose to preselect the way in which students will articulate their new understandings—perhaps through written work, oral presentations, or multimedia creations.

As you become more comfortable with the inquiry process and students become more skilled, you will likely begin working with a *blended* model of inquiry. You decide when and where to give student autonomy and where it may be necessary to step in to explicitly teach the required skills. Blended inquiry is the form of inquiry most often attempted in classrooms since it allows for a balance of and flexibility in teacher and student direction.

At some point in your course you may choose to use an *open* model of inquiry. Students choose the question, and design and conduct the investigation independently. In this case, multiple inquiries are being conducted on different topics at the same time. Obviously, students must be highly skilled and experienced in inquiry in order to undertake this type of inquiry.

Moving from a model of guided inquiry to open inquiry requires a gradual release of responsibility from teacher to student:

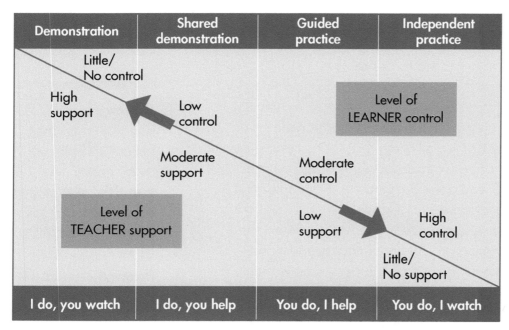

FIGURE 43: **Gradual release of responsibility**

2. Plan on having students work together at least some of the time

One of the fundamental qualities of inquiry is that students work together to make sense of a question or problem as part of a democratic community of learners. Outside of school, we rarely learn in isolation. Few of us work at jobs where we function completely independently. It makes sense to have students work together as often as possible so that they can help each other to succeed, and so that they learn to cooperate rather than compete.

You may choose to have students work together for the duration of an inquiry, for parts of an inquiry, or for peer review and/or formative assessment. If you want students to work together for parts of an inquiry only, you may choose to select from the following tasks:

- Generate an inquiry question
- Determine a probable answer to an inquiry question and plan a research path

One of the fundamental qualities of inquiry is that students work together to make sense of a question or problem as part of a democratic community of learners.

- Select and analyze sources
- Evaluate and synthesize evidence
- Peer evaluate at any stage of the inquiry

You may also decide that you would like students to conduct their inquiry in groups. Groups may be assigned according to ability level (heterogeneous or homogeneous groupings), their interest in a particular inquiry question, or by personality type (a mix of personality types, including at least one extrovert and one introvert, is usually helpful).

3. Select or create powerful questions

In order for inquiry-based learning to work effectively in your classroom, students must start with a good inquiry question that excites learning and focuses on the big ideas of a discipline.

A good question is one that:

- generates thought (rather than recall);
- comes from a point of debate or confusion within a discipline;
- encourages students to think in a way they may never have before;
- invites deep feelings, as well as deep thought; and
- leads to more questions, rather than answers.

Examples of strong inquiry questions for the disciplines of social studies, civics, history, and geography include:

- If I didn't live in Canada, would I want to?
- Can we continue to live as we do with the resources we have?
- Can we justify the sacrifices made by Canadians for war and conflict?

4. Create an assessment plan

Assessment bridges teaching and learning. Assessment identifies where the learner is going (by establishing and sharing big ideas, concepts, fundamental skills, related learning goals, and success criteria with students); where the learner is right now in their learning (by observing students, having conversations, and assessing products); and how to get the learner to their goal (through the use of peer, self-, and teacher feedback).

While that may appear to be a simple formula, the real challenge is to create a realistic assessment plan (where you don't mark all night and every weekend) that maintains focus on the important learning goals in the course, provides more time for dialogue and feedback to students and between students, and gives you and the student the confidence to say what learning has occurred and to what degree.

The following summary is a helpful guide to this process:

- ☑ Early in an inquiry, introduce students to the chosen summative product (e.g., photo essay, political "rant," essay, social media product, debate, etc.).

- ☑ Ask students to discuss what they know about this product. Provide more information as needed.

- ☑ Ask students to think about what criteria they would determine are needed to make an excellent product versus a mediocre product.

- ☑ Generate and share ideas as a whole class. Record answers on the board. Refine as needed. Post the final version in the classroom and ask students to refer to it often as a means of peer and self-assessment.

- ☑ As the course progresses, teachers can post student products that exemplify quality in all or some criteria.

5. Gathering evidence of learning

In order to collect valid evidence of learning during an inquiry, you can intentionally triangulate the data that you collect while considering the feedback you will give to provide next steps for student learning. The three areas of triangulation are conversations, observations, and products.

Conversations are moments when student and teacher and student and student reveal their thinking to each other. Listening carefully to student voices will help you consider what understanding the student is demonstrating at all stages of problem solving and inquiry.

Observations occur when we attend carefully to students with specific learning goals and criteria in mind. You can observe a student taking notes, summarizing text, making a presentation, and collaborating with their peers.

Products tend to be more formal pieces of assessment data. These are data that we have structured to take a snapshot of the student's ability at a certain point in time. Products enable you to assess a number of skills and/or a cluster of curriculum expectations and goals.

By increasing our assessment repertoire beyond a single source of evidence (e.g., products), and by using triangulated assessment data, you can be more confident of the validity of your assessment. This is because students may reveal their understanding and demonstrate their learning at times and in ways that are not always revealed in formal products.

6. Allow time for students (and you) to reflect, revisit, and reimagine

As teachers, we have all kinds of pressures to meet timelines and deadlines. We have reporting deadlines, curriculum requirements, and if we team-teach, we often have to proceed through the curriculum in a lock-step fashion with other teachers of the same course. But when we worry too much about moving along according to a schedule, we take away the opportunity for our students to engage in rich, deep thinking.

The inquiry process helps teachers apply the brakes by affording students frequent opportunities to reflect on their learning and loop back to reconsider, revise, and restructure their thoughts. Reducing the volume of tasks and providing more time for reflection increases the chances that students will come to understand more not only about the world, but also about themselves as thinkers and learners.

When we worry too much about moving along according to a schedule, we take away the opportunity for our students to engage in rich, deep thinking.

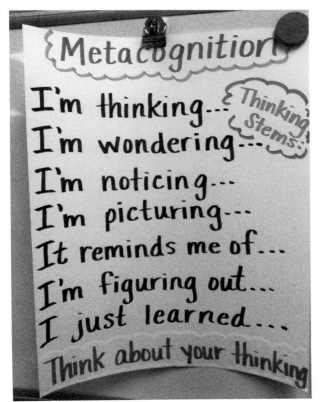

FIGURE 44: Anchor charts can encourage metacognition in the classroom

Source: Courtesy Amanda Kendall, author of The Teaching Thief Blog, http://theteachingthief.blogspot.ca/

We cannot overemphasize the importance of stopping and reflecting on our classroom practice; it is as important for us to do as it is for students to reflect on their learning.

7. Create the essential vocabulary to communicate inquiry thinking

Communication is the only way that students can make their learning visible to you and to other students. This will require the integration of inquiry vocabulary into your daily classroom tasks. Over time, you should notice a new and powerful common language being spoken by your students that will accelerate their ability to move towards independent inquiry. The following strategies will help you to develop such a vocabulary amongst your students:

☑ Create "anchor charts" or "word walls" of key inquiry vocabulary. Students can provide sentences in their own words that demonstrate the meanings of the words. Post them in conspicuous places in the classroom. Refer to them and revise them often.

☑ Have students complete an inquiry journal where they articulate their understanding of two to three key inquiry vocabulary words in relation to their learning, not as discrete terminology.

☑ When listening to collaborative groups at work, ask questions that invite students to explain their understanding of key inquiry vocabulary in relation to the work they are completing.

☑ When conferencing with students regarding their inquiry work, probe their understanding of key inquiry vocabulary.

☑ Have students collaboratively create metaphors for key inquiry vocabulary words. Show them how to apply their understanding of inquiry thinking and thinkers to life outside the classroom.

☑ Students can create T-charts, Venn diagrams, or other key visuals to define key inquiry vocabulary words or to compare two or more key inquiry vocabulary words.

☑ Create inquiry vocabulary "check-ins" by asking students comprehension and application questions. You can create the questions, or another option would be to have students create questions on specific terms to assess their peers.

8. Help students make sense of their evidence and data

Today's students can access digital information that was previously unavailable, such as museum and archive collections. This opens up a huge range of possible topics and issues for exploration. On the other hand, digital access has also resulted in a deluge of information that is overwhelming for adults, let alone students. Students will benefit if you provide them with some key points to help them sift their results:

☑ Consider the author/source and the date of publication.

☑ Be suspicious of websites that have a number of errors.

☑ Be suspicious of websites that do not list any information about the creator of the site and what would qualify him or her to write about the topic.

☑ Check the backlinks (an incoming hyperlink from one website to another) for the website.

These four points can form the basis of fundamental criteria that students use to assess websites. In order to provide descriptive feedback, you would—through conversations, observations, or a written product—determine to what extent the students understand and are using the criteria. In other words, you can help students by specifying criteria and by providing specific and timely feedback.

9. Identifying patterns and trends in evidence

Once students have gathered and analyzed individual sources, they need to synthesize their evidence and information to draw conclusions. This can be a challenge for students, but one way you can help them is to have them identify patterns or trends in the information they have located. (Patterns or trends are ideas, themes, or arguments that repeat throughout the evidence.)

Students can be prompted to identify patterns and trends through questions such as the following:

■ What is similar about this evidence?

■ Are there two or three points or arguments that are consistent across a number of pieces of evidence?

- Does a timeline of the evidence show that people are more concerned about this issue or less concerned about this issue than in the past?

- What does a growing or declining trend tell me about the issue under investigation?

- Is the theme reflected in more than one data source?

- Are smaller patterns contained within the themes? If so, what are they?

- On closer inspection, what evidence is not a good fit? Why?

10. Drawing conclusions based on the evidence

Some students will struggle when trying to conclude their inquiry. But at the most basic level, drawing a conclusion is really about weighing the pros and cons of an issue. Tools such as a basic PMI chart will help students to draw conclusions based on their evidence.

One of the goals of inquiry is for students to understand that the conclusions they make about the inquiry question should be based on the evidence they find, the prior assumptions they held, and the connections they were able to make between the various pieces of information they studied. Another student working from a different group of sources might come up with an entirely different conclusion. This is to be encouraged because it shows that students understand that the "answer" is dependent on a number of factors. The "answer" is the result of the inquiry, moving students away from a transmissive approach to learning, which posits that all students should get the same answer to the same question.

Furthermore, it can result in a very rich lesson if two or more groups of students have explored the same inquiry question and come up with very different conclusions. As their findings are shared with one another and the class, these differences provide additional avenues for questioning, considering, and deep thinking.

At the most basic level, drawing a conclusion is really about weighing the pros and cons of an issue.

7.2 Looking back, moving forward

Although teachers have always had to deal with change, we currently face a situation where the learners in our classrooms have changed quite dramatically. They have grown up in a digital world. We know from research on the brain that reading and viewing digital materials from an early age actually changes the way the brain is wired (Jabr, 2013; Killian, 2009; Nielsen, 1997). While we may—or may not—lament these changes, this is our reality.

Our students today don't process information in a linear fashion. They are used to reading and viewing in snippets. Their attention spans are short. And although they are comfortable using technology, they still lack basic research and analysis skills, and are not born knowing how to write, synthesize, or reflect. Just like our younger selves, they need to be taught these skills.

An inquiry model of instruction allows educators to meet the diverse needs of the students in our classrooms. It allows students to work on questions of interest to them, while we work to teach them the critical skills and big ideas that underpin our disciplines.

It may well be that the role of the teacher is more important than ever as individuals, communities, and societies deal with the rapid change that has resulted from emerging technologies, immigration, and globalization.

Whether we choose to introduce the inquiry model in a small way in our classrooms by trying it for one unit or one project at a time, or whether we try to employ this instructional method in a more systematic way, inquiry allows us to draw on the key elements that exist in all learners: curiosity and a desire to think, debate, and explore. These natural human traits are the trump cards of effective teachers.

An inquiry model of instruction allows educators to meet the diverse needs of the students in our classrooms.

REPRODUCIBLES

REPRODUCIBLE 1: How to Model and Assess Inquiry Dispositions

Inquiry disposition	What it looks like in the classroom	How inquiry-based learning supports this disposition	Student reflection prompts
Curiosity	Teacher and students want to know more about the world and its people. They ask important, relevant, and deep questions. These questions are not answered easily—nor does the student or teacher have the correct answer in mind at the outset. They are honestly perplexed by the issue/question/problem and have the motivation to uncover a possible answer/solution.	Inquiry-based learning begins with a question, a curiosity, or a wondering related to the discipline.	An important and relevant question that I find interesting and related to the topic we are studying is… I think it is important to answer this question because… This question is challenging to answer because…
Self-confidence	Teacher and students trust that they can figure out difficult problems by using their reason and intelligence.	Inquiry-based learning proceeds when learners trust that they can harness their own skills of reasoning when confronted with a challenging question.	Even though I may face difficulties or make mistakes, I believe I can succeed in this inquiry because… When faced with a problem I cannot initially answer, I feel that…
Flexible thinking	Teacher and students are willing to try out different types of thinking (i.e., political thinking, creative thinking, critical thinking, and reflective thinking) and different points of view.	Inquiry-based learning allows students to develop discipline-specific thinking skills as they collect, critically assess, and evaluate sources, and then generate conclusions.	I have used critical thinking in this inquiry to… The thinking skill that I have found most helpful in this inquiry is…
Open-mindedness	Teacher and students are genuinely interested in other perspectives and attitudes. They realize that the question is never fully answered and that knowledge is always being constructed. They are open to continual learning.	Inquiry-based learning demands that evidence is gathered from multiple sources that represent diverse perspectives.	Multiple sources and diverse perspectives are important to consider in this inquiry because… When I talk with others, I think the argument I agree/disagree with the most is… because… The one perspective I am having difficulty finding evidence to support is…

Inquiry disposition	What it looks like in the classroom	How inquiry-based learning supports this disposition	Student reflection prompts
Perseverance	Teacher and students are not put off by obstacles and challenges in their learning.	Inquiry-based learning is challenging. It demands higher-order thinking and communication skills.	What I find challenging about this inquiry is.... The strategies that I will use to move my inquiry forward are...
Taking risks	Teacher and students are not looking for one correct answer, but are more playful and creative in thinking. They are confident that their thinking is a "work in progress" and are open to new ways of thinking and learning that may be outside their area of expertise/comfort/skill.	Inquiry-based learning is an adventure. It is typically not a linear process, but one with twists and turns. These intellectual surprises allow students to experience what true experts in the discipline feel when attempting to answer a question or solve a problem.	I feel that this inquiry could have many different answers because... I have tried new strategies such as... to research, examine, and communicate my understanding of this inquiry.
Reflection	Teacher and students think about their thinking and know why it is important to do so. They can self- and peer assess products. They can make connections to their personal lives and identity as well as to the broader world.	Inquiry-based learning is complex. Reflection during an inquiry allows learners to consider how to face a challenge, how to meaningfully assess their work and the work of others, and how to make meaningful connections between what they are learning in an inquiry and their lives.	At this point of the inquiry, I am exceeding/meeting/not meeting the success criteria because... The areas I need to improve in are... The strategies I will use to meet my goals are...

SOURCE: Adapted from Walsh, J, and Sattes, B, *Thinking Through Quality Questioning*, Corwin Press (2011).

REPRODUCIBLE 2: Inquiry Rubric

Name: _____   Date: _____

Goal: To design and conduct a successful inquiry and to communicate the results.

Curriculum Expectations: _____

Final Product: _____

Success Criteria Categories*	High degree of effectiveness	Considerable effectiveness	Some effectiveness	Limited effectiveness	Further support required
Inquiry skills and processes **The student will** ask and refine relevant questions that further the investigation gather and analyze multiple sources critically evaluate evidence and make valid conclusions					
Application of thinking skills in proposing a course of action **The student will** transfer critical, creative, and discipline-based thinking skills when proposing an answer to the inquiry question or proposing a course of practical action					
Communicate new understandings **The student will** communicate clearly communicate persuasively engage the audience use the vocabulary and terminology of the discipline					
Learn what is currently known about the topic/problem **The student will** demonstrate knowledge and understanding of content important to the inquiry					

*Success Criteria: Success criteria should be co-constructed between teacher and student as appropriate. Success criteria answer the question "What are the specific characteristics of a successful inquiry?"

REPRODUCIBLE 3: Inquiry Assessment Planning Template

Teacher: _____ Class: _____

Task: _____

Inquiry Domains: What a student needs to know and do during an inquiry	Ways to gather evidence of student learning		
	Products	Observations	Conversations
Inquiry skills and processes Student asks and refines relevant questions that further the investigation. Student gathers and analyzes multiple sources critically. Student evaluates evidence and makes a valid conclusion.			
Application of thinking skills in proposing a course of action Student transfers critical, creative, and disciplinary thinking skills when proposing a course of practical action.			
Communicates new understandings Student communicates clearly. Student communicates persuasively. Student engages the audience. Student uses the vocabulary and terminology of the discipline.			
Learns what is currently known about the topic/problem Student demonstrates knowledge and understanding of content important to the inquiry.			

REPRODUCIBLE 4: Asking Questions about Photographs

Name: _____ Date: _____

Inquiry focus: _____

Work collaboratively through the following steps to try to create deep questions based on your thinking about the photograph.

1. Have a discussion about what you observe is happening and what you infer is happening.
2. Each person in the group should create 3 to 5 questions based on your curiosities arising from the photograph.
3. After everyone has a list of preliminary questions, collaborate to choose 3 of these initial questions to "perfect" them into deep inquiry questions.
4. For each of your "perfected" questions, list 2 or 3 additional questions that arise from the perfected questions.

---

1. This is what we see in the photograph (observations):

_____

This is what we infer from what we see in the photograph (inferences):

_____

2. My questions about the photograph:

_____

3.

Our top 3 deep inquiry questions	Do our 3 questions meet these criteria for a deep inquiry question?
1.	❑ An invitation to think (not recall, summarize, or detail). You can't find the answer through a simple Internet search. ❑ Requires support and justification, not just an answer. ❑ Open-ended; typically there is no final, correct answer.
2.	❑ Arises from genuine curiosity and confusion about the world. ❑ Makes you think about something in a way you never considered before.
3.	❑ Invites both deep thinking and deep feelings. Asks you to think ethically (what is right and wrong). ❑ Leads to more good questions.

4. Additional questions that arise from the deep inquiry questions:

_____

REPRODUCIBLE 5: Asking Questions about Sources

Name: _____ Date: _____

Speaker/Source: _____

Answer the following questions individually.

1. What is your purpose in asking questions of this person or source?

   _____

   _____

2. What are your questions?

   _____

   _____

3. What types of questions have you asked?

   _____

   _____

Answer the following questions in a group.

4. Compare your questions with those of other students. What points of view and assumptions do the questions reveal?

   _____

   _____

5. How do the questions link to important concepts and content that we have discussed?

   _____

   _____

6. How could you improve one of your questions?

   _____

   _____

Name: _____ Date: _____

Individually reflect on the following quotes and answer these questions.

1. Consider what ideas in the quotes you agree with and provide examples of the quotes' relevance to your life inside and outside the classroom. Use the questions at the bottom of the page to stimulate your thinking.
2. Think about why questioning will be important in this classroom and how we can improve as questioners.
3. Join with a partner to discuss your thoughts. Note how your conversation with a partner was different after thinking about questioning.

"The most important question in the world is, 'Why is the child crying?'" **Alice Walker**

"The power to question is the basis of all human progress." **Indira Gandhi**

"It is better to debate a question without settling it than to settle a question without debating it." **Joseph Joubert**

"Life's most persistent and urgent question is, 'What are you doing for others?'" **Martin Luther King Jr.**

"The question isn't who is going to let me; it's who is going to stop me." **Ayn Rand**

"If love is the answer, could you please rephrase the question?" **Lily Tomlin**

"A wise man can learn more from a foolish question than a fool can learn from a wise answer." **Bruce Lee**

"The great question that has never been answered, and which I have not yet been able to answer, despite my thirty years of research into the feminine soul, is 'What does a woman want?'" **Sigmund Freud**

1. What concept is at the root of these quotes?
2. Some of the quotes are asking questions. What "type" of question is being asked? Ethical? Political? Social? Philosophical?
3. What does the person being quoted believe is the importance of questions?
4. Which quotes resonate with you and why?
5. Which quotes trouble you and why?

Name: _____ Date: _____

Inquiry focus: _____

As you work through the inquiry, use these questions to focus your thinking and to assess the quality of your thinking.

Questions that unpack the inquiry

1. Why do we care about this issue?
2. What do we hope to find out?
3. How will we proceed to answer the question/solve the problem?

Questions that unpack concepts

1. What is the main idea you are using in your thinking?
2. Can you explain the concept clearly to another person?
3. Is there a different concept that would work in considering this problem?

Questions that unpack evidence

1. What is the source of this information?
2. What is the quality of this information?
3. Do I have all the information I need?
4. How am I making meaning of this information?

Questions that unpack reaching a conclusion

1. What does the author or speaker take for granted?
2. What am I taking for granted?
3. What alternative assumptions are there to consider?
4. What are the relevant points of view?
5. What is my point of view?
6. Can I explain my thinking?
7. How did I reach my conclusion?
8. Have I considered other alternative plausible conclusions?
9. What is this argument/conclusion/point of view leading us?
10. What will happen if my conclusion is correct?

REPRODUCIBLE 8: Questioning Skills Rubric

Name: _____ Date: _____

Inquiry focus: _____

Success Criteria Category	Exceptional	Good	Getting there	Not yet	Further support required
QUESTIONING **Inquiry Question** The student asks relevant questions that further the investigation.	Student applies understanding of the qualities of an effective inquiry question by consistently asking (and refining) inquiry questions.	Student applies understanding of the qualities of an effective inquiry question by frequently asking (and refining) inquiry questions.	Student applies understanding of the qualities of an effective inquiry question by asking (and refining) some inquiry questions.	Student is beginning to identify the qualities of an effective inquiry question but cannot yet apply their understanding to refining or asking their own inquiry questions.	Student needs further support in asking inquiry questions.
Questioning Thinking The student answers analysis questions accurately (i.e., identifying concepts, purpose, point of view, inferences, and assumptions) and refines their thinking based on their analysis.	Student consistently answers analysis questions accurately, refines their thinking, and sets reasonable learning goals based on their analysis.	Student frequently answers analysis questions accurately, refines their thinking, and sets reasonable learning goals based on their analysis.	Student sometimes answers analysis questions accurately, refines their thinking, and sets reasonable learning goals based on their analysis.	Student is beginning to accurately answer analysis questions, refine their thinking, and set learning goals based on their analysis.	Student needs further support in answering analysis questions accurately and setting reasonable learning goals.

Descriptive feedback and next steps:

My goals related to this feedback:

Name: _____ Date: _____

Inquiry action words

question	To request information
clarify	To make something easier to understand
extend	To expand a meaning
defend	To speak or write in favour of a person, idea, or action
refute	To prove that something is wrong
assess	To evaluate the quality of (synonym: to evaluate)
analyze	To examine in detail to expand meaning
synthesize	To combine ideas to form a theory (overall explanation)
evaluate	To judge based on criteria (synonym: to assess, but often construed as a more demanding and exacting form of assessing)
persuade	To convince someone of your way of thinking
conclude	To infer on the basis of evidence

Words to describe thoughts, beliefs, and ideas

logical	Clear, sound reasoning
coherent	Logical and consistent
effective	Capable of producing desired result
clear	Easy to understand, not confusing
precise	Exact, accurate, careful
reliable	Trustworthy
abstract	Something that is not a material object, typically an idea
concept	An idea that is connected to something abstract
practical	Connected to real situations rather than ideas or theories Likely to succeed if implemented
theoretical	Ideas on which a subject is based (rather than practical)
ethical	Beliefs about what is right and wrong
operable	Something that can be used
accurate	Correct and true
relevant	Closely connected to the subject under consideration
significant	Important enough to have an effect or to be noticed

Concepts important to inquiry-based learning

inquiry	Asking questions and collecting information/evidence to answer the question
metacognition	Knowing about knowing (or thinking about thinking)
bias	To show prejudice
point of view	A particular attitude or way of considering
perspective	A mental view or outlook
implication	A possible effect or result of an action
assumption	A belief that something is true although there is no proof

Words to describe inquiry dispositions
(from *Reproducible 1: How to Model and Assess Inquiry Dispostions*)

curiosity	Teacher and students want to know more about the world and its people. They ask important, relevant, and deep questions. These questions are not answered easily, nor does the student or teacher have the correct answer in mind when they begin. They are honestly perplexed by the issue/question/problem and have the motivation to uncover a possible answer/solution.
self-confidence	Teacher and students trust that they can figure out difficult problems by using their reason and intelligence.
flexible thinker	Teacher and students are willing to try out different types of thinking (i.e., political thinking, creative thinking, critical thinking, and reflective thinking) and different points of view.
open-mindedness	Teacher and students are genuinely interested in other perspectives and attitudes. They realize that the question is never fully answered and that knowledge is always being constructed. They are open to continual learning.
perseverance	Teacher and students are not put off by obstacles and challenges in their learning.
taking risks	Teacher and students are not looking for one correct answer but are more playful and creative in thinking. They are confident that their thinking is a "work in progress" and are open to new ways of thinking and learning that may be outside their area of expertise/comfort/skill.
reflection	Teacher and students think about their thinking and know why it is important to do so. They can self- and peer assess products. They can make connections to their personal lives and identity as well as to the broader world.

REPRODUCIBLE 10: Today's Discussion Exit Card

Name: _____   Date: _____

Topic being discussed: _____

1. How did you contribute to today's discussion? Add a comment beneath the choices that you check off.

   ☐ I asked a question that related to a preceding idea.

   _____

   ☐ I made a comment that showed interest in what someone else said.

   _____

   ☐ I made a connection between two ideas.

   _____

   ☐ I used body language to support other speakers.

   _____

   ☐ I built on someone else's thoughts.

   _____

   ☐ I disagreed in a respectful way.

   _____

2. What one important idea from today's discussion changed your thinking?

   _____

   _____

   _____

3. Think about the class as a whole. What can we do to improve the quality of our discussion?

   _____

   _____

   _____

Name: _____ Date: _____

Individually reflect on the following quotes and answer these questions.

1. Consider what ideas you agree with, and provide examples of the quotes' relevance to your life inside and outside the classroom.
2. Think about why listening will be important in this classroom and how we can improve as listeners.
3. Join with a partner to discuss your thoughts. Note how your conversation with a partner was different after thinking about listening.

> *"When I get ready to talk to people, I spend two thirds of the time thinking what they want to hear and one third thinking about what I want to say."* **Abraham Lincoln**

> *"People love to talk but hate to listen. Listening is not merely not talking, though even that is beyond most of our powers; it means taking a vigorous, human interest in what is being told us. You can listen like a blank wall or like a splendid auditorium where every sound comes back fuller and richer."* **Alice Duer Miller**

> *"This is the problem with dealing with someone who is actually a good listener. They don't jump in on your sentences, saving you from actually finishing them, or talk over you, allowing what you do manage to get out to be lost or altered in transit. Instead, they wait, so you have to keep going."* **Sarah Dessen**

REPRODUCIBLE 12: Listening Self-Assessment

Name: _____ Date: _____

Topic being discussed: _____

Complete this reflection following a lengthy discussion in a collaborative group.

I maintained eye contact with the person speaking.

Yes!   *Most of the time*   *Not yet*

My facial expressions and body language communicated interest, openness, and respect.

Yes!   *Most of the time*   *Not yet*

I was quiet when others were talking and I did not interrupt.

Yes!   *Most of the time*   *Not yet*

I paraphrased other people's ideas and used their ideas to make connections to my own ideas.

Yes!   *Most of the time*   *Not yet*

I avoided, as much as possible, "inner chatter" in my mind that interferes with attentive listening.

Yes!   *Most of the time*   *Not yet*

Next steps:

_____
_____
_____
_____
_____
_____
_____
_____
_____
_____

REPRODUCIBLE 13: Fishbowl Observation

Name: _____ Date: _____

Topic being discussed: _____

You have been chosen to observe a group conversation carefully (like watching fish in a fishbowl).

For the following criteria, record one specific example that you observe. Be prepared to provide specific and respectful feedback to the group following your observation.

1. Participants build on each other's thinking.

   _____

2. Participants are respectful of each other.

   _____

3. Participants encourage alternative points of view and perspectives.

   _____

4. Participants engage in active listening (eye contact, body posture, giving verbal acknowledgements of each other's points).

   _____

Note any challenges that the collaborative group faced and suggest a strategy for improvement.

_____

_____

_____

_____

How can you apply this experience as a fishbowl observer to your own listening and oral communication skills?

_____

_____

_____

_____

REPRODUCIBLE 14: Listening Critically to Media

Name: _____ Date: _____

Topic being discussed: _____

Media source and date: _____

Speech or political commentary

1. Who is the speaker?

2. Who is the intended audience? What is the purpose of the speech/commentary?

3. What is the main idea or argument presented?

4. Describe the speaker's use of voice (tone, pace, pitch, use of pauses).

5. Describe the speaker's use of body language (eye contact, facial expression, body posture).

6. If you were this speaker's oral communication coach, what advice would you give them?

Panel discussion/Debate

1. Who are the speakers?

2. Who is the intended audience? What is the purpose of the panel/debate?

3. What is the main idea or argument presented by each speaker?

4. Choose one speaker and complete the following questions:

    a. Describe the speaker's use of voice (tone, pace, pitch, use of pauses).

    b. Describe the speaker's use of body language (eye contact, facial expression, body posture).

5. Who was the most effective speaker? Consider both the speaker's ideas and their communication skills in your answer.

News report

1. Who is the target audience? What words, sounds, or images suggest this?

2. How many speakers are featured in this report? Are different points of view represented?

3. What part of the story is not being told?

4. Whose point of view carries more weight in the story? How do you know?

5. Consider the impact of visuals and sound effects in persuading and engaging viewers.

IQ: A Practical Guide to Inquiry-based Learning

REPRODUCIBLE 15: Assessing My Point of View on a Topic

Name: _____ Date: _____

Record the inquiry question you have selected and think carefully about everything you currently know or believe about the topic. For each point you record, think about where you learned the information or formed your belief, and how it might impact your research on this inquiry question.

Inquiry question:_____

1. a) One thing I know or believe about this topic: _____
   _____

   b) Where did I learn this? _____
   _____

   c) How might this impact my research? _____
   _____

2. a) One thing I know or believe about this topic: _____
   _____

   b) Where did I learn this? _____
   _____

   c) How might this impact my research? _____
   _____

3. a) One thing I know or believe about this topic: _____
   _____

   b) Where did I learn this? _____
   _____

   c) How might this impact my research? _____
   _____

4. a) One thing I know or believe about this topic:
   _____

   b) Where did I learn this? _____
   _____

   c) How might this impact my research? _____
   _____

REPRODUCIBLE 16: Trustworthy Websites for Gathering Sources

Name: _____ Date: _____

Canadian Museum of Immigration at Pier 21, www.pier21.ca
Primary sources have been bundled on topics that include:
- War Brides
- Jewish War Orphans
- British Evacuee Children
- Immigration

CBC, www.cbc.ca
Current events and in-depth news features can be found on this site. It is a public site and there is no fee or limit on how many articles, videos, or podcasts can be viewed.

CBC Archives, www.cbc.ca/archives
This is an archive of older news clips from television and radio broadcasts. These primary sources capture historical events as they unfolded. The clips are short, so your students will be able to quickly find out if particular clips will help them to address their inquiry question. The information on the website has been organized by general categories (e.g., Environment, Health, Politics, and Economics) and some of it has been organized by more specific topics, called WebQuests (found under "For Teachers"). Some of these WebQuests include:
- The Internment of Ukrainians in Canada
- Counting the Costs (Canada and military conflict)
- Preserving Métis History
- The Mackenzie Valley Pipeline
- Compensation (mercury poisoning in the Grassy Narrows community)

Library and Archives Canada (The Learning Centre), www.collectionscanada.gc.ca/ education/008-2010-e.html
The Learning Centre created a list of great sites for both younger children and teenagers that link to many content topics in Canadian classrooms. A sample of topics includes Art, History, Social Studies, Literature, and Science. All of the websites referenced have been vetted as appropriate for young learners, and are age- or grade-appropriate. The only downside to this site is that the Learning Centre is no longer being updated.

Saskatchewan Archives, www.saskarchives.com
Primary sources have been bundled on a variety of Canadian history topics including:
- The Regina Riot
- The Great Depression
- Sod Houses
- Homesteads

IQ: A Practical Guide to Inquiry-based Learning

Name: _____   Date: _____

Use this template to analyze each of the sources you have gathered up to this point in the inquiry process.

Name of source: _____

Type of source: _____

Source	Criteria for evaluating evidence
Source	Where did it come from?
Objective	For what purpose was it created?
Usefulness	Is it relevant to the inquiry question under investigation?
Reliability	Is it accurate, unbiased, and reliable?
Context	Is it supported by other evidence?
Evidence	What does it prove?

Source: Adapted from schoolhistory.co.uk

Name: _____ Date: _____

Use this template to assess whether you have enough evidence to start answering your inquiry question.

Inquiry question: _____

Source	Support	Challenge	Both

Do you have sources that represent a variety of perspectives and points of view on the inquiry question?

REPRODUCIBLE 19: Evaluating and Drawing Conclusions—Reflecting on the Inquiry Question

Name: _____   Date: _____

Use this template to organize your evidence according to the arguments made by your sources.

Inquiry question: _____

Content focus of our investigation: _____

Evidence in support of argument 1:	Evidence in support of argument 2:	Evidence in support of argument 3:	Evidence in support of argument 4:

Our overall conclusion:

Additional thoughts/recommendations:

Name: _____   Date: _____

Use this template to weigh the pros and cons of the question you are investigating.

Inquiry question: _____

+

The positives

The negatives

▬

Interesting

REFERENCES

Chapter 1

Barell, J. (2003). *Developing more curious minds.* Alexandria, VA: Association for Supervision and Curriculum Development.

Berliner, DC and Calfee, RC (eds.). (1996). *Handbook of educational psychology.* New York, NY: Macmillan.

Freire, P. (2000). *Pedagogy of the oppressed: 30th anniversary edition.* New York, NY: Continuum Books. (Original work published 1970)

Greeno, J, Collins, A, and Resnick, L. (1996). Cognition and learning. In Berliner, DC and Calfee, RC (eds.), *Handbook of educational psychology* (15–46). New York, NY: Macmillan.

Jang, H, Reeve, J, and Deci, EL. (August 2010). Engaging students in learning activities: It is not autonomy support or structure but autonomy support and structure. *Journal of Educational Psychology 10*(3), 588–600.

Jennings, L and Mills, J. (2009). Constructing a discourse of inquiry: findings from a five-year ethnography at one elementary school. *Teachers College Record 111*(7), 1583–1618.

Kuhn, D, Black, J, Keselman, A, and Kaplan, D. (2010). The development of cognitive skills to support inquiry learning. *Cognition and Instruction 18*(4), 495–523.

Martin-Hansen, L. (February 2002). Defining inquiry: Exploring the many types of inquiry in the science classroom. *The Science Teacher 69*(2), 34–37.

McComas, WF. (n.d.). *Enhancing the Education of Scientifically Gifted Students with Inquiry Instruction* [PowerPoint slides]. Retrieved from http://coehp.uark.edu/pase/Inquiry_Science_Instr2.pdf

Neville, AJ. (2009). Problem-based learning and medical education forty years on. *Medical Principles and Practice 18*(1), 1–9.

Palmer, S. (2002). Enquiry-based learning can maximise a student's potential. *Psychology Learning and Teaching 2*(2), 82–86.

Shymansky, JA, Hedges, LV, and Woodworth, G. (1990). A reassessment of the effects of inquiry-based science curricula of the 60's on student performance. *Journal of Research in Science Teaching 27*(2), 127–144.

Spronken-Smith, R, Walker, R, Batchelor, J, O'Steen, B, and Angelo, T. (February 2011). Enablers and constraints to the use of inquiry-based learning in undergraduate education. *Teaching in Higher Education 16*(1), 15–28.

Vajoczki, S, Watt, S, Vine, MM, Liao, X. (January 2011). "Inquiry learning: Level, discipline, class size, what matters?" *International Journal for the Scholarship of Teaching and Learning 5*(1).

Chapter 2

Growing Success: Assessment, Evaluation, and Reporting in Ontario's Schools. (2010). Ontario Ministry of Education.

Hattie, J. (2008). *Visible learning: A synthesis of over 800 meta-analyses relating to achievement.* Oxon/New York, NY: Routledge.

Walsh, J and Sattes, B. (2011). *Thinking through quality questioning: deepening student engagement.* Thousand Oaks, CA: Corwin Press.

Wiggins, G. (September 2012). Seven keys to effective feedback. *Educational Leadership: Feedback for Learning 70*(1), 10–17.

Wiliam, D. (2011). *Embedded formative assessment.* Bloomington, IN: Solution Tree Press.

Chapter 3

Barell, J. (2003). *Developing more curious minds.* Alexandria, VA: Association for Supervision and Curriculum Development.

McTighe, J and Wiggins, G. (2013). *Essential questions: opening doors to student understanding.* Alexandria, VA: Association for Supervision and Curriculum Development.

Paul, RW and Elder, L. (2000). *Critical thinking: Basic theory and instructional structures handbook.* Tomales, CA: Foundation for Critical Thinking.

Paul, RW and Elder, L. (2010). *The Miniature Guide to the Art of Asking Essential Questions.* Tomales, CA: Foundation for Critical Thinking.

Chapter 4

Hein, G. (October 1991). *Constructivist Learning Theory.* Retrieved from http://www.exploratorium .edu/ifi/resources/research/constructivistlearning .html

Lipton, L and Wellman, B. (2003). *Mentoring matters: A practical guide to learning focused relationships.* Sherman, CT: Miravia.

Chapter 5

Adolescent Literacy Guide: A Professional Learning Resource for Literacy, Grades 7–12. (2012). Ontario Ministry of Education.

Canadian Investigations: Civics and Citizenship. (2014). Don Mills, ON: Oxford University Press.

Seixas, P and Morton, T. (2013). *The big six historical thinking concepts.* Toronto, ON: Nelson.

Seixas, P and Colyer, J. (February 10–12, 2011). Annual general meeting of The Historical Thinking Project. Toronto, ON.

Wineburg, S. (Fall 1991). On the Reading of Historical Texts: Notes on the breach between school and academy. *American Educational Research Journal,* 495–519.

Wineburg, S, Martin, D, and Monte-Sano, C. (2013). *Reading like a historian: teaching literacy in middle and high school history classrooms.* New York, NY: Teachers College Press.

Chapter 6

Donohoo, J. (2013). *Collaborative inquiry for educators. A facilitator's guide to school improvement.* Thousand Oaks, CA: Corwin.

McKenzie, J. (October 1999). Students in resonance. *From Now On: The Educational Technology Journal.* Retrieved from http://www.fno.org/oct99/ resonance.html

Murdoch, K. (2012). *Inquiry learning – journeys through the thinking processes* [PDF]. Retrieved from http://kathmurdoch.com.au/uploads/media/ inquirylearning.pdf

Wiggins, G. (June 10, 2010). What is a big idea? *Authentic Education.* Retrieved from http://www .authenticeducation.org/ae_bigideas/article .lasso?artid=99

Chapter 7

Jabr, F. (April 11, 2013). The reading brain in the digital age: The science of paper versus screens. *Scientific American.* Retrieved from http://www .scientificamerican.com/article.cfm?id=reading -paper-screens

Killian, L. (Spring 2009). New textual formats: Reading online is re-wiring the human brain and changing how we process information. *Dalhousie Journal of Interdisciplinary Management 5,* 1–13.

Nielsen, J. (October 1, 1997). *How Users Read on the Web.* Retrieved from http://www.nngroup .com/reports/how-people-read-web-eyetracking -evidence/

INDEX

PHOTO CREDITS